MASTER DIRECT SELLING

A Pitch Your Prospect Cannot Reject

Srinivas S N

ISBN 979-8-88772-969-5

This book is dedicated to the Almighty, who has been a light and guided me through whatever I have done to date. It is because of His blessings I am what I am today. I would like to thank Him for guiding me and making me a better human being and for inspiring me to write this book and to help others succeed in life.

Contents

Acknowledgement

From the bottom of my heart, I would like to thank the following people who have stood by me and inspired me to write this book.

My father for always being my hero. Thanks, dad, for all that you have done.

My mother for being a great inspiration to me throughout my life and for the unconditional love that you have given me until this moment.

All my teachers and my gurus for sharing all the knowledge with me and many others without expecting anything back in return.

To the Almighty for guiding me and giving me the opportunity to positively contribute to the betterment of society.

This part of my book and my life will never be complete without thanking my wife, my daughter, and my son. You have all been such wonderful support in my life, and it is only because of your support and continuous words of encouragement that I was able to achieve all that I have achieved. I thank you all for having trust and confidence in me.

Thank you all.

Introduction

Many people whom I have come across working in sales tell me that 'sales' is the most challenging job to be done. Many people even after knowing that they are getting into one of the toughest jobs don't have proper training in sales from their organisations or their managers. In this book, you will be able to understand very clearly what sales mean, and what are the dos and don'ts in sales. When you complete reading this book you will become a thorough professional in sales and you will be able to sell anything. I am sure that this sounds interesting.

When I started my career in sales two decades ago, it was a time when training and development as a department was not very prominent in our country nor were the availability of trainers and coaches to help the new hires to understand the process of the tricks of the trade as they are available today. The training that was provided to me both on the product and the selling skills part was imparted by my manager. Yes, I did learn from him, and went ahead and executed what he asked me to do without any questions asked. It worked for me as I believe it does for many of you. I am sure our managers would have learnt the same from their managers and along with experience evolved as better salespeople. Having said this, I did not really know if that is how it was supposed to happen. Is this a proven method? Are these the best ways of selling a product? The most important thing that was running through my head was why should I do this a particular way I was asked to do it. I mostly did not get an answer to that question.

Are you feeling the same way? Don't worry you are not alone. Many salespeople go through similar feelings.

Then as I moved into training and development in my career, I was forced to ask this question to myself. I started seeking answers to questions that I didn't have an answer to when I was doing my job in sales. I did this because my current role as a trainer demanded me to do this. I could not face people in a training programme without having an answer to the question of "Why am I supposed to do this? Why this way? and many more". This made me uncover more information about the art and science of sales and selling skills. Then I went on to execute a lot of training programmes on sales across the country for more than a decade. I thoroughly enjoyed my stint as a corporate trainer in sales. I was blessed to be associated with many industries like telecom, hospitality, BPO, and construction, and currently as a consultant to top corporates. This decade of experience in sales training made me understand that immaterial of the industry that one works, the selling process is the same with a few changes done to the process as per the industry requirements. In simple terms, the science part of selling is the same. This is what unfortunately many salespeople are not aware of. If they were aware of these secrets everyone in sales would be a successful salesperson. That is why I say, **not every sale is successful but everyone can be a successful salesperson.**

So, if you are a person who is in sales, an entrepreneur, a businessman or a person who wants to get into sales and become successful read this book thoroughly. I would recommend you read it at least a couple of times to understand the ocean of knowledge that this book has to offer although it is compiled together in a short package.

I would also like to make this very clear to each one of you who are reading this book that I am nowhere claiming that I have come up with this module of selling or I invented it. I am just putting across information that is currently available in different places, perhaps in different books by different authors or in different places including your own company. I am writing this book with all the knowledge that I gained during my career in sales and later as a corporate sales trainer and coach. I am writing this book so that you will be able to understand sales and selling in a much more detailed manner. When you complete reading this book, I assure you that you will be a completely changed salesperson. I would say a more professional salesperson.

PART I

FUNDAMENTALS OF SELLING

In any vertical of a professional career if you want to be successful you need to be a master of the fundamentals of that vertical. Unfortunately, this is what is missing with many people as they think that the fundamentals of that business or that vertical are very easy to learn, or that they already know it, so why should we waste time or put more effort into learning the fundamentals? It is way too easy.

Sales is no different as I already told you many of us would have learnt sales from our superiors and we either do it the same way or would have evolved as a salesperson with experience. So, there are many chances that we are not fully aware of the fundamentals of sales or selling. So, this does not make them or us a professional in my humble opinion. So first let's get into understanding the fundamentals of sales and selling.

Even before we get there, let us first understand a few things which will come in handy as we read more. First, try answering this question: According to you who is a professional? Many believe a professional is a member of a profession or any person who earns a living from a specified professional activity. The term also describes the standards of education and training that prepare members of the profession with the knowledge and skills necessary to perform their specific roles within that profession. In addition, most professionals are subject to strict codes of conduct, enshrining rigorous ethical and moral obligations. The abovementioned is a simple explanation that you can find on Wikipedia.

If you ask me who is a professional, I would say, "A person who is professional in anything he does for a living and when he can answer the questions on what, when, how, where, and why about a thing which will fetch him the desired outcome". Now go back and ask yourself once again if you are a professional in sales or in selling. Many people know the answer to the first four questions: what, when, how, and where. Unfortunately, they don't have the answer to the last question: why they are supposed to do it? Now this book will also majorly focus on the why part, as I want every one of you to be a professional salesperson once you complete reading this book.

Let's start with the easiest thing about selling. Is selling an art or a science? I know it's very easy, but don't get fooled because all fundamental questions sound that way but they are the toughest questions to answer. Take your time. Before I explain in detail, my next question is, "What is art?" and "What is science?" Yes, yes, I know it's getting easier, and you are thinking that selling is very easy. I would also agree if you can hold your thoughts just until you finish reading this book completely.

According to Wikipedia, art is a diverse range of human activity and resulting product that involves creative or imaginative talent expressive of technical proficiency, beauty, emotional power, or conceptual ideas. There is no generally agreed definition of what constitutes art, and ideas have changed over time.

Wikipedia explains science, on the other hand, as a systematic enterprise that builds and organizes knowledge in the form of testable explanations and predictions about the universe. The earliest roots of science can be traced to ancient Egypt and Mesopotamia from around 3000 to 1200 BCE.

Now try asking yourself the same question again is selling art or science? I will now tell you my thoughts on this, in very simple terms, if you follow a defined process and the result or the outcome does not change, then it's science. When you follow a defined process and the outcome or the result changes then it is art. I am very sure it is a simple way to understand and remember this. Many people, when I ask them if selling is an art or science, they pick either one of them. I would very confidentially say that selling is neither an art nor a science but a combination of both art and science. Because in selling there are defined processes that you need to follow which do not change, but how you execute those processes vary from person to person and also, very importantly the outcome or the result of the selling process can never be the same. So selling is neither art nor science but it's a combination of art and science in it.

CHAPTER ONE

Fundamentals of Sales and Selling

Now, the fun is about to start as we are going to jump deep into topics related to sales and selling. Selling is not easy. If it was every salesperson on this earth would have been successful.

Now let us understand two different terminologies in detail: sales and selling. First, let us think and focus on understanding what is sales and what is selling. Even people in sales have not been able to answer this question perfectly.

"Sales are activities related to selling or the number of goods sold in a given targeted time. The delivery of a service for a cost is also considered a sale." (Source: Wikipedia)

When you google on the internet you will find many interesting answers to this; I picked one for you: "Selling is any transaction in which money is exchanged for a good or service. If the buyer wishes to strike a deal, they will give the seller an agreed-upon amount of money in exchange for the seller's product/service. Put simply, selling is the act of persuading."

Now, this is where it becomes a little tricky as the term selling also comes up in the definition of sales. But we know that sales and selling are not the same. So how it is different and how to understand it in a much simpler form?

If you ask me to explain what sales and selling are all about in very simple terms I would say the following:

> "Sales can be defined as an exchange of goods or services for an amount of money or its equivalent, which involves the act of selling."

> "Selling is a process of identifying the need and wants of a prospect and presenting the product in a tailor-made fashion to satisfy the want."

Sale is a concept of the exchange of goods or services for an amount of money whereas selling is customer or prospect related which happens in different ways and forms.

CHAPTER TWO

Sales Fundamentals and Concepts

Now in this chapter, we will understand more in detail the fundamentals and concepts of sales. If you do not have this knowledge, you can never be a professional in sales. As I always say, only if your fundamentals are strong, you will be successful in whatever you do. Now let's relate this with an example, let's say you want to build a house. What is the point in spending a lot of money on the interiors of the house and the look of the house if you are not willing to get the foundation of the building correct? Like the foundation is the most important part of the building, so are learning and the fundamentals and concepts that are the most important part of selling, the rest all comes later.

When you are in sales it's very important to learn the following terminologies that are frequently used but many times not understood in the correct manner. So, please focus on and understand the following terminologies very clearly before moving on.

- Need
- Want
- Demand
- Features
- Advantages
- Benefits
- WIIFM

Need

Dr. Philip Kotler, American marketing author, consultant, and professor emeritus, who is also considered the Father of Modern Marketing, defines need "as the state of deprivation of some basic satisfaction. Ex: food, clothing, safety, shelter."

Unfortunately, this has been interpreted in different ways or in a completely incorrect manner. Let me share with you my interpretation of this definition. I feel that need is a basic requirement for human existence like hunger and thirst. No one can create hunger or thirst, it is just felt. So the very common saying "create a need for the product before you sell it is wrong"—need cannot be created.

Want

Dr. Philip Kotler defines wants as the desire for a specific satisfier of need, e.g.: Indians want foods like paneer tikka and tandoori chicken, etc. Americans want food like hamburgers and French fries.

Now, this is very self-explanatory but I will share a few more examples on the same. Let's say that you are feeling thirsty the need is thirst. Now the choice that you make individually to quest the thirst is called want. For example, I would like to have a glass of water, while you might prefer to have Pepsi while another person would like to have a glass of buttermilk. Now please understand that the common factor we all had was thirst, which is a need. The individual's choices are called wants. So you cannot create a need for a product but you can create a want for a product or service.

Demand

Dr. Philip Kotler defines demand as a want for a specific product backed up by the ability and willingness to buy.

To understand this let's look at the same using an example. Let's say that you are thirsty, which means that the need for thirst has been raised. Now when you make a choice to drink a bottle of Pepsi or buttermilk, it means the want for a particular product arises as well. Now if you have the ability and the willingness to pay for the product then only the demand for the product is there. The demand for the product does not arise only if you have the ability or only the willingness to pay for the product or the services. You should have both the ability and willingness to pay for the product or services; many times people will only have one among the two.

Features

Every product or service has features in it. Features can be very simply explained as facts or characteristics about the product or services. These are things about your products or services that do not change instantly. Let's for example say you are referring to a pen then the design of the pen is called one of its features. So a product or a service can have multiple features.

Advantages

All the products or services have advantages. Let's understand this more clearly; advantages are related to features directly. Your product's features turn out to be an advantage when the features of your product have something superior to the features that are offered by competition or competitors. If your product's features do not have anything superior when compared to the competition then the feature stays as a feature and does not become an advantage. So there are no guarantees that all the features that are there in your product/service will turn out to be an advantage.

Benefits

Benefits are something that each and every salesperson should know about in detail. When you make a sales presentation talking about your product's features and advantages the client is subconsciously asking himself what do I get out of this? So when you can answer this question then the feature or the advantage becomes a benefit to the prospect. If you cannot provide a personal answer to that question then the feature or the advantage remains just that, nothing more. Remember not every feature and advantage of your product or service can become a benefit to the prospect. It is completely individualistic.

Clients buy the product or services from you for their benefit and not for their features and advantages. So ensure to present the benefits rather than the features and advantages.

WIIFM

When you are giving a sales presentation to a prospect he/she will be subconsciously asking themselves what they are going to get out of the feature or the advantage. This question that runs in their head is called the WIIFM—"What is in it for me?" If you can answer this question of WIIFM, during the sales presentation to the prospect then the feature or the advantage becomes a benefit else it just stays as a feature or an advantage. Now for you to make them (the prospect) understand that the feature or the advantage is a benefit to them, you will have to explain to them how it would be beneficial for them by telling stories.

Most successful salespeople are the best storytellers. So start working on your ability to tell stories. Please, remember telling a story is different from telling a lie. I am asking you to tell stories and by no means asking you to lie in a sales presentation.

Chapter Summary/Key Takeaways

So, in this chapter, we saw the various fundamental concepts and terminologies that are used in sales. These are the building pillars of your selling skills. If you are not clear, I would recommend you read through the chapter again. Don't be in a hurry to understand. "Rome wasn't built in a day".

So, let's quickly summarize the key takeaway points that we understood in this chapter. Some of the important aspects of selling that we covered were: need, want, demand, features, advantages, benefits, and WIIFM.

In the next chapter, you will understand in detail the science part of selling and why it's very important.

PART II

SEVEN STEPS OF SELLING

In this chapter, you will understand the science part of selling and the process that needs to be followed to be a successful salesperson. As we have already seen selling is a combination of both art and science. It's very important for us to understand both of them simultaneously and in detail. To understand this we should know that there is a process that is involved in selling and we cannot change the process or the sequence of doing something. In simpler terms, it means you cannot change the process of selling because if you do so, then you are changing the science of selling and that will not get the desired outcome. So, let us first understand the sequence of selling.

The sequence of selling is defined below, and it involves seven steps.

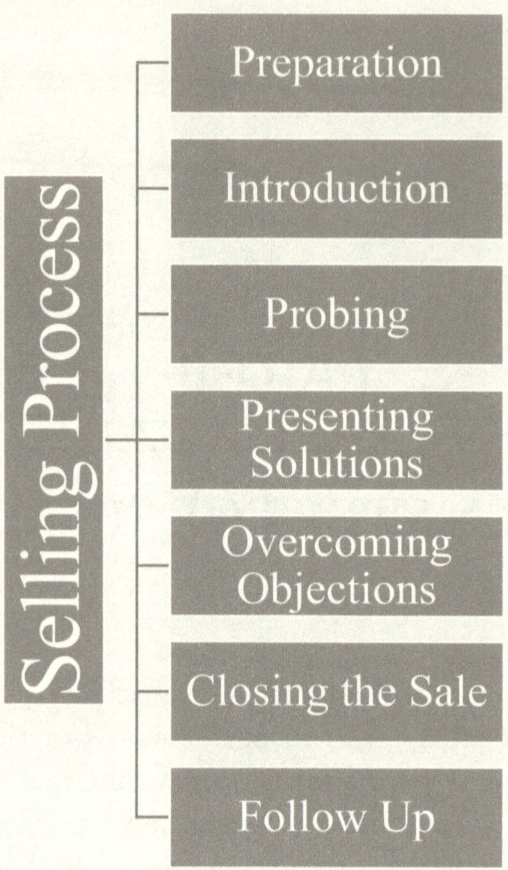

The above-mentioned is the defined sequence of any selling process, be it a product, or service that you are trying to sell. The process of selling does not change; it is pre-defined. Many salespeople make the mistake of altering the selling process which is the major reason why they tend to fail in selling. The first thing to remember is that don't ever try to alter or change the sequence of selling no matter what.

The same seven steps of selling can also be broadly classified into three major categories.

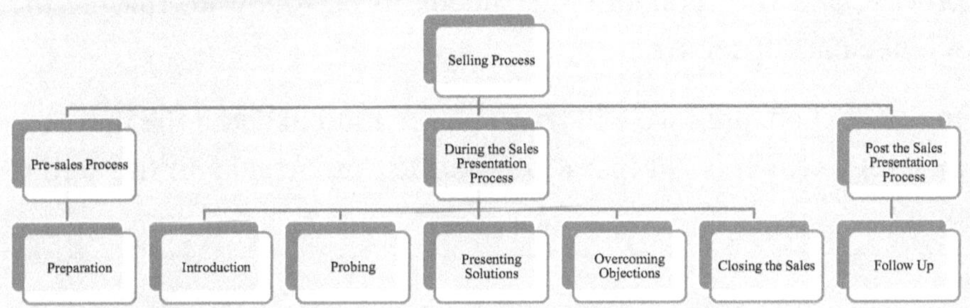

1. **Pre-sales Process**: Anything that happens before meeting the prospect in person.

2. **During the Sales Presentation Process**: Anything that happens while interacting with the prospect in person.

3. **After the Sales Presentation Process**: Anything that happens after interacting with the prospect in person.

So, the science part of the selling process is very clearly stated and defined. Please understand that if you want to be successful in selling, don't try to alter the steps or the sequence of the selling process. This is the thumb rule that needs to be followed while trying to sell any product or service to a prospect.

Chapter Summary/Key Takeaways

In this chapter, we have understood the seven steps of the selling process and the sequence that needs to be followed, that is, the science part of selling.

In the next chapter, we will try to understand in detail the first step in selling which is "Preparation" and its importance in the selling process.

CHAPTER THREE

Preparation

When I normally start my presentation on this topic in sales training programmes a lot of people tell me that this is the easiest part of selling—let me assure all my readers that it is not, it is just assumed to be that way. Many times, in life, we don't concentrate on the fundamentals because we tend to believe that it is easy, or that we already know it. As many experts say if your fundamentals are strong then it is easy to build on them. If your fundamentals are not strong, then there is no point in having great knowledge of the add-ons.

Understand Your Company in Detail

It is very important for all the sales personnel to know about the company that they represent in detail. As a salesperson, you should understand the company and the brand that you are trying to sell because only when you know this in detail you will be able to convince the prospect to buy the product or services from your company. Understand that there are options available for the prospect to buy a product or service as there is a lot of competition in the market nowadays. A wide range of options is available in front of the prospect. When a prospect wants to buy any product or service the first thing that they would look at is, from which company to buy the product or the service. Hence, for the prospect to buy the product you need to convince the prospect that your company is the right choice for him or her. To do this, learn the following about your company:

1. History of the company

2. The company's vision statement

3.   The mission statement

4.   The USP of your company

Understand the USP of Your Product

You need to understand the USP of the product or the service that you are selling. Let's first understand what USP is. Many salespeople tend to believe that the full form of USP is "Unique Selling Point", but it is not. The full form for USP is actually "Unique Selling Proposition". Now let's understand what USP is. Most of the products or services that you will be selling will have many features and advantages. But what is its most unique feature or its USP? It means that this feature should not be available with any of the competitors, and is something that is unique about your product or service. So be very clear that the USP of your product or service is a feature that is available only with your product/service, and it is not available with any of your competitors. Let's look at this with an example.

Let's say you are working with a real estate company trying to sell their apartments or villas and if your company says that they have 50 different amenities offered in the apartment which no other competition offers then the number of amenities in the apartment becomes the USP of that apartment that you are trying to sell. If any other competitor has 50 or more than 50 amenities in their apartment, then it means that having 50 amenities is no more the USP of that apartment.

Practise Doing Your Sales Presentation

This is something that every salesperson must do throughout their career. I have seen many salespeople starting their careers with this, but this habit seems to vanish away as they gain experience. I am not sure why. I think many believe that because they have the experience they don't need to practice. What a joke! Look at all the professional sports people who have been successful in their careers. Even the best in the world like Sachin Tendulkar, Roger Federer, and Michel Jordan even during their prime spent most of their time practising what they were good at, nay, what they were best at. WHY? Didn't they have enough experience? They did. But they excelled and ruled their respective sport because they practised more than their colleagues and competitors in that sport. That is why they were the best. If you want to be the best salesperson or if you want to be successful in selling then you need to practise your sales presentation, again and again, day in and day out no matter how many years of experience you have in selling. This is what differentiates the best from the rest. While practising your sales presentation focus more on the opening statements of your sales pitch, which we will see in detail in the next chapter "Introduction".

Understand Your Products FAB in Detail

What's FAB? It is your product's features, advantages, and benefits. It's very important as a salesperson to understand your products or service's FAB in detail. You will have to concentrate on learning all the features—what advantages and benefits do they offer to a prospect? You need to focus on this and ensure that you know them by heart. For this to happen you need to do lots of research and it's also very important for you to make this a habit. Not many salespeople do this as they tend to think that they can read out the features from the brochure. Please understand that the best salespeople use the brochure only as a reference tool and they show it to the prospect or hand it over to the customer and post the sales presentation for the customer's reference. If you don't know about your product's FAB, how can you expect the prospect to believe what you are saying? Do you think you will be able to build confidence in the prospect? I don't think so. So, if you want to be a successful salesperson then ensure that you spend a lot of time understanding your product's FAB.

Understand Your Competitor's FAB in Detail

It is not enough if you know only your company's FAB; it is also important to know your competitor's FAB. This is what really differentiates between the average and the best sales personnel. The average salesperson will know about his competitors. But the best sales personnel would always know what their competitors have to offer in detail. They would know all about them, in fact, know more about their competitor's products/services as compared to their own products or services. Many sales persons would depend on the internet to gain information on what their competition has to offer. That is not enough. Get on the field, pose as a prospect, and understand how the competition is pitching their product. What is that they are communicating to their prospects and how are they presenting their features, advantages, and benefits? After all, we are not discussing selling the product or services over the internet. Most people prefer a personal connection with some person from the organization before they buy the product. Yes, I agree even though times are changing and online sales are the way forward, you still need to remember that machines cannot replace the human element. NOT YET. So, buckle up and hit the field, visit all your competitors, not only the primary but also your secondary competitors and understand them in detail. It's time-consuming and very hard. But success isn't easy to come by and it's true of sales too. If you want to be successful in sales, then you need to put in the extra effort. After all, you are rewarded well enough through incentives and many more perks that are offered to the sales personnel that aren't offered to the other employees working in the same organization.

Ensure That Your Sales Kit is Complete and Ready

For any professional to be successful in their line of activity they need to ensure that their kit is ready, well-maintained, and organized to be used. As salespeople, you should ensure that your sales kit is ready, well maintained, and organized well enough according to the sales flow. You need to ensure that the sales kit is organized sequentially. How would you know it? I am sure by this time you would have put in a lot of effort in practising your sales presentation so you would know by heart what would be required and when. Always think what are the tools that you would require during the sales presentation with a prospect. How will it be beneficial for them? Why are you using it?

So, let us look at what is included in the sales kit. Though this would change from industry to industry most of the things would be common enough. The sales kit should have

- Working pens
- Business cards
- Business card holders
- Company and product brochures
- Technical manuals
- Calculator
- Price list
- Availability chart
- Deodorant (I would not recommend a perfume)
- Mouth freshener
- Shoe shiners

In case there are specific things that are needed in your industry or organization specific then feel free to add them to the list and get ready.

Chapter Summary/Key Takeaways

In this chapter, we saw the importance of being well-prepared for your sales presentation and how to go about it. As the saying goes the more you practise in peace for war the less you will bleed in war. Yes, sales and selling are a day-in and day-out profession; so prepare for it well enough if you want to be successful. Let us recap on what are the things that we covered on this topic.

- How and why it is important to understand your company in detail?

- How and why it's important to understand the USP of your product or service?

- How and why it is important to understand your product or services' FAB in detail?

- How and why it is important to understand your competitor's FAB in detail?

- How and why it is important to practise your sales pitch?

- How and why it is important to ensure that your sales kit is complete and organized sequentially?

In the next chapter, you will learn in detail about the second step of the selling process which is "Introduction".

CHAPTER FOUR

Introduction

In this chapter, we will be looking at what are the things that need to be done during the process of "Introduction" in a sales process or during a sales pitch. Generally, an introduction is the first step of the selling process. This step sounds very easy as it generally does not last more than a few minutes. That is the reason why many sales persons believe it's very easy when compared to the other six steps in the selling process. As I always say don't judge too early. The introduction seems to be very easy on paper, but you must know exactly what to do and how to do it. If you fail here in this step, then no matter how hard you try you will not be very successful in selling the product or service. That is for sure.

Ensure That You Are Groomed Well

Before the start of the sales pitch or before meeting the customer, you should ensure that you are well-groomed. First impressions make lasting impressions. This is what I have learnt in sales. I have also understood that making a good first impression is easier than changing the first impression about a person. Understand that subconsciously we tend to be more comfortable and believe a person who is well groomed when compared to a person who is not so. Being the brand ambassador of your company, it is your responsibility to create a good first impression with the prospect. Be very careful as you are not only trying to impress the prospect personally but also professionally. The prospect based on your appearance will form impressions about you and your organization. Many times, this is not revealed by the prospect.

Do you know how long it takes for a person to form a first impression of another person? The impression that you form about someone as soon as you meet them for the first time is called the first impression. And this will be based on many aspects. Now let's come back to the question of how long does it take for a person to form an opinion about another person after meeting the person for the first time? Many researchers have done their studies on this topic, and many agree that first impressions about a person are formed between seven and 45 seconds of seeing a person or interacting with a person for the first time. Yes, you did read it right, all it takes is less than a minute for us to form an opinion about another person. So, remember you only have less than a minute to impress a person or ensure that you have helped a person to form a good opinion about you.

Some might ask, "What if I am not able to form a good first impression?" Is there a second chance? Do you know how long it takes to form a second opinion about another person or how long it takes to change your first opinion? Well, you will be surprised to know that people tend to change their first impression about a person only after 45 minutes of interacting with that person. Now let us look at this from sales perspective. Will you always get 45 minutes with a prospect? The answer would be many times "No". So, what happens if you don't get the opportunity to change the first impression that was formed in the mind of the prospect? So, he leaves with the first impression that you have set about yourself and your organization. This is also one reason why many people say that first impressions are lasting impressions as many times we don't get 45 minutes with the prospect. Hence, I always believe that it's very important to do it right the first time. Impress your prospect within the first seven seconds and create good first impressions.

Now let's look at how to do it.

First thing is that you should ensure that you are groomed well. I would always recommend professional attire for the sales team unless there is a uniform advised for the sales team personnel by the management of the company. Now let's look at how to be well groomed. Ensure that

- your hair is properly cut and combed.

- you are neatly shaved.

- your nails are trimmed and maintained properly.

- you use deodorant.

- you're wearing a belt that matches the colour of your shoes.

- you are ready to greet the prospect with a smile.

Meet and Greet the Customer Professionally

Now we are ready to meet and greet the prospect.

Imagine now you are going to meet the prospect in person—either you would meet the customer in your office, or you would meet them at their premises. Sometimes you might meet the customer in a commonplace too. But wherever you meet the prospect you must be ready to impress the prospect within the first seven seconds but don't take too much pressure on yourself. Be ready for the show and be willing to enjoy what is going to follow. Many salespeople tend to focus more on converting the prospect into a customer in simple terms they would focus on sales conversions, here I would like to say don't focus on the result, just focus on the process. If you get the process correct mostly the result will be as expected.

When you see the prospect, walk towards them slowly and steadily. Don't rush toward the prospect. Maintain a steady pace. Always maintain eye contact and smile. Don't forget to smile this is the most important part. Ensure the smile is real and don't fake it. Remember the prospect will be able to distinguish between a real smile and a fake one.

Offer a Professional Handshake

Once you have come close to the prospect ensure that you maintain good proximity but don't get too close. Now offer them a professional handshake.

The below picture gives you insights into how to offer a professional handshake should be.

Ensure your wrists are straight and don't squeeze the prospect's palms. Hold the prospect's palms gently and shake their hands not more than three times. I would recommend two times is the best count to shake hands. One is too little and more than three would not be advisable.

Introduce Yourself

As you are offering a handshake it's very important to introduce yourself. Start by wishing the customer; the best way is to start with "Good Morning", "Good Afternoon", or "Good Evening" as per the time. Many people get the greeting wrong because they don't notice the time. Don't do this mistake. Understand that you are a professional and professionals don't make silly mistakes and they are always ready.

So, while greeting the customer greet them as per the timing:

"Good Morning" when you greet a client from 12 am to 11.59 am.

"Good afternoon" when you greet between 12.00 pm and 3.59 pm.

"Good evening" when you greet a client from 4.00 pm to 11.59 pm.

Don't do the silly mistake of greeting the prospect by saying "Good Night". I know you are thinking who would do such a silly thing, but believe me, I have seen some sales personnel making this mistake. So please don't do it. Small things do make a huge difference.

Introduce yourself with your full name followed by your designation in the company. I have seen a few sales personnel not quoting their designation while introducing themselves to the prospect. This tells the prospect that they are not confident about their job and their position in the system. Even if you are at the entry level, it is very important to show them that you are the person in charge. You should mean business and you should be proud of who you are in the company.

While Meeting a Group of People...

There might be instances where you will be meeting a group of people in your sales presentation instead of just a single client. Let's look at this with an example, let us say you are selling a car or real estate. The buying decision is made by more than a couple and the people who are making the buying decision would be different and the wants of every individual would be completely different. Here now let's say that you are meeting a family who has come to meet you. While you are introducing yourself first introduce yourself to the person/prospect whom you have been in touch with until then. Then immediately focus on the senior citizens if they are present in the group, then move towards the women in the group, and finally greet the children too. While greeting the entire group you need not introduce yourself again, however, keep smiling and greet them as per the time, which we have discussed already. Now greeting every member of the group is necessary and important. Please don't even miss a single person in the group because I am sure that you would agree that you will not be able to judge who is the decision maker and who are the influencers in the group otherwise. So, treat every person with respect and importance. Don't prejudge any person.

Don't Make Any Physical Contact With Kids in the Group

I have seen many sales personnel while meeting the prospect for the first time, when there is a child or children in the group, they would tend to bend down towards them and pinch the cheek and then greet the child. I would say that this is a big NO, NO. Don't do this even if you are doing it without any bad intentions. Let's look at this from the prospect's point of view. The prospect is meeting you for the first time and if you suddenly get close and personal with their child and moreover if you try to touch them physically, your clients will get uncomfortable, don't you think? So always remember during this stage of the conversation don't try to touch the child or the children in the group.

Maintain Good Proximity to the Prospect

You need to maintain good proximity between you and the prospect. Ensure that you don't get too close to them at the same time don't be too far away from them. I would suggest about one foot and a half or two feet distance between you and the prospect would be the ideal distance. Getting too close regarding the proximity again would not put the prospect in a comfortable spot. During the entire course of the sales presentation always look at how things are happening from the prospect's point of view.

Offer Your Business Card to the Prospect

Now the time has come to offer your business card. Understand that the first official document that you are offering to the prospect from you and your company's end is your business card. So, offer the business card with respect and with style. People love to do business with salespersons with a positive attitude and style. So, I recommend you buy a very good business card holder and carry your business cards in it. Take the business card from the business card holder in front of the customer and hand it over to the prospect. If it's a family that you are meeting then it's ok if you hand over a single business card to the main member of the family or the person with whom you have been interacting. In case you are officially meeting a group of people from a different company, or you are doing a B2B (business to business) meeting, then hand over the business card to each one present in the group.

Follow the Mirroring Technique

Now let's look at a very interesting technique in sales called "the mirroring technique". The mirroring technique is where a person copies or imitates the body language of the other person standing in front of them. Psychologists say that people are more comfortable and at ease with a person who has a similar body language to theirs. So now in selling to make the prospect more comfortable with you I would recommend you mirror or copy the top half body language of the prospect for a few seconds and only for a few seconds and not more than that. Don't make this obvious to the prospect. Remember you are a professional who is playing a part. So do your role with utmost confidence and style. Also, remember that you are supposed to mirror the body language of the prospect only if they are either neutral or defensive body language and do it only for some time. I would recommend that you keep it to less than one minute. Again, I am warning you that should not do this in a manner it becomes obvious to the prospect. Understand that you are doing this only to put the prospect at ease and make them feel comfortable with you and the new environment that they are in. You don't want them to think you are mimicking them or teasing them.

Follow the Lighthouse Technique

In case you are doing a presentation to a group of people, it is very important to follow the lighthouse technique. Let's understand the lighthouse technique in detail—like how the light in the lighthouse keeps moving continuously in a circle you should continuously keep looking at each member of the group. Don't keep looking too long at a single person, keep looking at all the members of the group. It is mostly advised to move in a circular manner, starting and ending with the same person. As you are doing this ensure that wear a smile on your face.

Don't Ask "How Are You Doing?"

I have seen many sales personnel starting the conversation with the prospect by greeting them for the day and immediately moving on to ask them, "How are you doing?"

I know you probably are asking what's wrong with the question. First, you must understand that you are meeting the prospect for the first time. You don't know much about the prospect. You don't know if the prospect is an emotional or an egotistical person. You might not know how his day has been so far. So why start the conversation with a question which can put you on the wrong foot? Let's say here the customer responds by saying "I am not feeling that great or something like that, what can you do? If I, were you, I would be left with no other option than to ask if he would like to reschedule the meeting for another day. Yes, I would do that because I would not like to continue with the sales presentation with a person who is not feeling well. Generally, if he is not feeling well, he might not be able to concentrate during the sales presentation. So, I would recommend you not ask this question while meeting the prospect for the first time and during the first part of the conversation. Again, think from the prospect's point of view always. If you want to be successful in sales, put the prospect ahead of everything.

Collect the Business Card From the Prospect

During this stage of the presentation if it's a B2B (business to business) or a B2C (business to customer) presentation the prospect would also offer his/her business card. Now it's always polite and nice to collect the business card from your prospect and read through the card. Concentrate and try to understand more about the prospect. What is his designation? Which industry does he belong to? Try understanding the prospect as a person. Once you do that, in your mind draw a plan of action on how to interact with the prospect based on his/her age, designation, and the company that he works for. Do this quickly; don't take too much time for this and make the prospect wait for you to start the conversation. Respect the time of the prospect. Time is the most valuable commodity. It's very important both for you and your prospect.

Do a Name Drop if Possible

During your conversation with the prospect, in case, you know someone from his/her organization who works at a senior level or a well-known personality or someone who you think both you and the prospect may know or recognize who has already bought your product or services and are happy about the purchase, drop their name at the start of the conversation. Understand that you are trying to build a relationship with the prospect and start a conversation. But when you do a name drop you must be sure that the person whom you are referring to in your conversation holds a senior position in the organization or a well-known personality that your prospect recognizes and are a happy customer with your company. Do not do a name drop of a customer who holds a junior profile or who is dissatisfied with your product or services. Remember, most people will go and ask for feedback on the product or services from the person whom you have mentioned, if that person is not a satisfied customer, then all your effort will mostly go in vain. You can do the same thing with the prospect if you are visiting his/her place. Just replace the person whom you are referring to as a co-worker with someone residing in the same location. This will also do the trick.

Be Ready and Enjoy the Presentation

The thumb rule to becoming a successful salesperson is to enjoy what you are doing. Yes, it's a stressful job, no doubt about it, but understand it's rewarding to be in sales at the same time. Knowing this, always relax while interacting with the prospect, whether over a call or in person. And be confident. Put away all the pressures and be willing to enjoy each moment. Most people fail in sales because they are not able to handle the pressure and at the same time many sales personnel carry a lot of baggage like their experience while doing a sales pitch. They would be preoccupied with previous results, the current sales score for the day, and numbers to be achieved for the month, quarter, and year. If your mind is already filled with so many thoughts, how will you be able to give your 100% to the prospect? I am sure you can't. So how can you expect the desired results?

Chapter Summary/Key Takeaways

In this chapter, we have understood what we are supposed to do during the introduction. Understand that this step will not last for more than a few minutes, yet this is one of the most important steps in selling. By now you would have understood that this step-in selling would step up the stage for the entire sales presentation and come what may you need to get this right.

- To put it in a nutshell, we learnt:
- How and why, you should ensure that you are groomed well?
- How to be ready to greet the customer professionally?
- How to offer a professional handshake?
- How to introduce yourself professionally?
- How to interact with a group of people?
- Why should you not try to touch the children in the group?
- How to maintain good proximity to the prospect?
- How to offer your business card to the prospect?
- How to follow the mirroring technique?
- How to follow the lighthouse technique?
- Why we should not ask "how are you doing?"
- How to collect the business card from the prospect?
- How to do a name drop if possible?
- How to be ready and enjoy the presentation?

In the next chapter, we will learn about probing, one of the most challenging steps in the selling process.

CHAPTER FIVE

Probing

Probing is one of the most challenging steps in the selling process. Many sales personnel do the mistake of talking about the product or services that they have to offer even before understanding the wants of the prospect. If you are one of those who are doing it, I would say that you are "telling" about your product or the service to the prospect rather than "selling".

Let's recap a little bit about selling. "Selling is a process of identifying the need of a customer and presenting the product in a tailor-made fashion to satisfy the need". Now if you have understood this in detail then you would agree with me that before you present your product or services you need to understand the wants of the prospect. Like always, put the customer first, ahead of everything if you want to be successful in selling.

Suspects, Prospects, Customers, and Consumers

Let us understand in detail the differences and similarities of some terms that we commonly use to denote in sales, like customer, prospect, suspect, etc.

Suspect: When you are meeting a person for the first time you might not be sure if the person has the want for the product or the service or if he has the demand for the product or service. You are starting a conversation without knowing much about this person, so you call him a suspect. We generally avoid using this term because of its legal connotation. But in sales parlance, it is common to use the word suspect and the meaning is very clear as stated above.

Prospect

Generally, after interacting with a suspect for some time and you conclude that the suspect has the want and the demand for the product or service that you are trying to sell then you move them to the category of a prospect. So, you will call a person who has the want and the demand for buying the product or services to be a prospect; however, understand very clearly that not all suspects are not prospects. Some might have the want but not have the demand. To be a prospect they should have both the want and the demand, or else they will only stay as a suspect.

Customer

Any prospect who ends up paying from his/her pocket to purchase the product or the services that you are offering is called the customer. Not all suspects and prospects will become your customers. Only the people who pay to use or buy your product or services are called customers.

Consumer

Generally, this is where a few people get confused. A consumer is a person who finally gets to use the product or the service. This might sometime not be the person who paid for it. There are chances that the customer and consumers can be different people.

Let's understand each of the above terms with an example. Let's say I am going to the salon to get a haircut. As I walk in, I am a suspect. Soon after interacting with the salesperson, I look at the price list and feel the pricing is steep. So I walk away as I don't want to spend so much. In that case, I leave as a suspect. Now if I go through the service card or the price list and decide the pricing is ok after interacting with the salesperson, but I am not very comfortable with other reasons like the décor, or the person who is going to cut my hair, etc. and therefore decide not to use the services then I become a prospect for them. If, on the other hand, I decide to go ahead and have my hair cut then I become a customer for them. If I had gone with my son and decided to get haircuts done for both, and I pay for both of us, then I am their customer and both my son and I become the consumers of the services offered by the salon.

Handling each one of these categories of people is different. Therefore, it is very important to understand the kind of person you are interacting with before you start selling.

Ask Permission to Start With a Few Questions

As a salesperson, always ask permission from the prospect to start with a few questions. Practise well in advance on what and how to question the prospect. A prospect is more interested in his/her wants, and he is interacting with you to see if your product or services offered will satisfy his wants. He is also curious to know how the product or service will satisfy his requirement. Or answer to the question of his WIIFM "What's In It For Me?". The common mistake that salespersons do is that they start bombarding prospects with questions without any preamble. Please understand that no one likes being questioned. So before questioning, ask for permission from the suspect or the prospect informing them politely that you require a few details on their requirement so that you would be able to provide them with all the necessary information on the product or service you are selling.

Write on Paper

I would always recommend the traditional way of writing down the information provided by the suspect or a prospect on a white sheet of paper. Always tell the prospect what you are doing and why you are doing it. For instance, you could tell them, "Sir, I don't want to miss any information that you are providing to me, so I am taking notes of those important details of your requirement. Hope it's fine with you." Usually, the prospects won't say no as they understand it's for their good and you are showing to the prospect that you are concerned about their requirement. In case a prospect says "No", it's ok. Simply smile, apologize, and move on. Normally taking down notes while you are interacting with the prospect shows that you are interested in their requirements and that you are not simply trying to sell a product. It also helps in remembering every detail about what the prospect wants.

People think that in sales it is important to improve verbal skills as opposed to listening skills. I beg to differ here. When you listen carefully, you will understand better what your prospect wants from your product or service. A change in tone, the use of certain words, and facial expressions will help you understand better your prospect's needs better. So listen and watch! And take notes whenever possible.

Probe But Don't Question

People, whether they are a suspect or a prospect, don't like overt questioning. As a salesperson, instead of questioning them probe them, which is more effective. "What's the difference?", you may ask. Let's look in detail.

Questioning

- Questioning is a technique that is commonly used to clarify or clear issues about a topic.
- Questioning is generally a one-way communication.
- There is not much emphasis on relationship building.
- Interviews are generally where you follow this technique.

Probing

- Probing is a technique that is commonly used by a person or an individual to dig deeper into the problem and get more information.
- Probing is generally a two-way communication.
- There is a lot of emphasis on relationship building.
- Sales/CRM personnel are always advised to probe the prospect or the customer to understand in detail the requirements or pain points.

Now that we have seen the difference, let's dwell a little deeper into probing in general because as a salesperson you need to probe the suspect or the prospect to understand their wants rather than questioning them.

Probe to Understand the Want of the Prospect

As a salesperson understand that each prospect is different and so are their wants. Don't assume that you know the prospect and why they are here to buy your product or your service. Let's say that you are trying to sell a car, now let's see what the different requirements of the prospect are. One may want to buy the car because of the brand, or the features available, for the comfort, mileage, and safety features, someone would like to buy a car for short drives to commute within the city, or just for long weekend drives... so the list goes on and on and on. Though the product or the service that you are trying to sell does not change according to the individual, the wants and the requirement for the product varies from individual to individual. So, probe to understand the requirement of the suspect or the prospect. Here if you dig deeper into the requirement of the prospect you would understand that it would be different to the requirement of each consumer, so understand who the prospect is and who the consumers are. What are the requirements of the prospect, and the consumers? And what are the requirements of the suspect because the prospect does not only buy the product for themselves but also spends the money to buy the product for the use of the consumers? If you are not able to convince the prospect that the product that you are trying to sell will satisfy the wants of both the prospect and the consumers, then mostly the sales will not happen. So again, I am reiterating the fact that you should clearly understand the requirement so probe in detail.

Probe to Build a Relationship

Many salespeople fail in probing or don't get the desired outcome because they don't do it right. They try to question the prospect rather than probing the prospect. Now to be able to probe the prospect, understand that you are probing to know the want of the prospect and to build a relationship with them. To be successful as a sales personnel you will have to be successful in relationship building. People buy a product or a service from a person whom they trust and rely on. So building a relationship is very important for that reason. Therefore, give importance to what the prospect says. Actively listen to their requirement. Ensure that the conversation is always maintained as two-way communication. Make sure that the probing and the conversation are not just product or service-centric. Yes, the main reason that you are probing the prospect is to understand his/her wants, but by probing you are using it as a tool to build a relationship with the prospect and make them trust you.

Keep it Light

One more reason why people fail in probing is that they tend to make this process a very serious affair. Don't do that. Keep the process light—add some humour, remember to smile, and maintain eye contact. Don't be very serious throughout the conversation. Though you are doing serious business it does not mean that you have to remain serious all the way through. People respond better to those with a good sense of humour. Psychologists say that people tend to spend more time conversing with those with a good sense of humour rather than with those who hold a straight face throughout the conversation. Now let me clarify here: keeping the conversation light is different from making the selling process a joke or making the process only fun-filled. All I am telling you is that if an opportunity arises to put your prospect at ease, then make use of it. Understand that it's only a skill set and if you work on it, you will be successful. For you to do that first you will have to understand the reason why you are doing it and practise how to do it. With time and effort, you will feel more comfortable doing it like everything else.

Show Empathy

While probing, the prospect will reveal their requirements and even their personality. There are high probabilities that they might share with you details of things that went wrong in their past while purchasing another product or service. They are giving you this information trusting you and they are also subconsciously telling you that I don't want that kind of experience again. Now here is an opportunity for you to build confidence in the prospect, and understand that the prospect is expecting you to know where he is coming from and what he/she has gone through. They don't want your sympathy but rather a show of empathy for what happened. So, give them what they want. Empathize with them. For this to happen you will have to understand the difference between empathy and sympathy because good empathetical probing will help you understand the want of the prospect, and understand better the prospect as an individual.

Let's understand the difference between empathy and sympathy:

- **Sympathy**: It is when you feel bad for someone, but you don't understand how they really feel about it. (The main emphasis is not on the feeling of the other person). A sympathetic approach would always have a surface-level understanding of the situation and more importantly, you relate to the situation from your perspective and not the other person's. Feeling sympathetic for a person or a situation will not help build relationships. Sympathy generally leads to advising on how to handle or react to the situation.

- **Empathy**: Empathy is the ability to understand the feelings of a person who has gone through a situation. When you empathize, you listen more actively without forming a judgement of the person as he shares the information. An empathetic approach will help you to connect with another person's feelings and emotions regardless of your personal experiences. Empathy allows you to discover the perspective of the other person and not yours. Empathy towards another person helps build better relationships.

Listen to the Prospect

We already discussed earlier that listening is not as easy as it sounds. To be a successful salesperson depends on how good a listener you are. Many people in sales have told me that you will have to be a good communicator to be successful in sales. I would only partially agree with that statement. To be a successful salesperson you have to be a good listener. I believe, "God has given us two ears and one mouth, God knows which is tougher."

So, let's now understand the different types of listening and how to be a good listener. In general, listening can be classified into eight types, which are as follows:

- **Informational listening**: It is used when you want to understand something about your client. It takes a high level of concentration and processing for the information received. This is generally practised while attending educational programmes, training, coaching and many more.

- **Discriminative listening**: This is the first listening type that humans are born with. Everyone subconsciously has this style of listening. You can clearly see this exhibited in babies, where the intention of a phrase is understood before understanding words. As adults, when you are listening to a conversation in a foreign language you would follow this type of listening. You normally use non-verbal cues to listen and analyze, like facial expressions, body language, and other mannerisms exhibited by the person sharing the information.

- **Biased listening**: This is also known as selective listening. Here people listen or hear only what they want to hear. This listening will mostly lead to the distortion of facts and information.

- **Sympathetic listening**: This type is more driven by emotion. More focus is given to the emotion and feelings of the conversation rather than the words used. The speaker will feel heard and vindicated when you use this style of listening. This type will help you build relationships.

- **Comprehensive listening**: Unlike discriminative listening, comprehensive listening requires language competencies. Several other types of listening are built upon comprehensive listening. Mostly comprehensive and discriminative listening goes hand in hand in workplaces and many walks of life.

- **Empathetic or therapeutic listening**: This style helps you to see other people's perspectives. Instead of focusing on the message, you tend to relate to the experience of the other person as your own.

- **Critical listening**: You use critical listening to analyze and process complex information. You use critical listening to evaluate what is being said. This type is very important when solving problems at the workplace or in personal situations. You use this type to analyze solutions offered by other people and decide if you agree with them or not.

- **Active listening**: Here you are ready to listen and respond by observing what verbal and non-verbal messages are being shared and then respond with the appropriate feedback. This builds conversations and relationships.

Use Open-ended Questions

If you need to be successful in probing and if you would like to build a good relationship with the prospect, then you must use more open-ended questions. To do that, you need to understand clearly what open-ended questions are and if there are any other types.

- **Open-ended questions**: In simple terms, open-ended questions are questions that cannot generally be answered with a "Yes" or "No" or with a static response. It generally is phrased as a statement rather than a question which enables a detailed response. An example of this is: "Where do you see yourself in the next 10 years?"

- **Close-ended questions**: Generally, these questions are replied to with a yes or no without a detailed response. Generally, close-ended questions are provided with options to choose a response from. Example: "Do you prefer coffee or tea?"

So, use more open-ended questions to probe the customer at the early stage of the conversation.

Paraphrase What You Have Understood

When you have started probing the prospect, they will generally start providing you with the required information; as this happens it's very important to paraphrase the received information. Now let me explain this in detail. Once the customer has shared some information, you should summarize your understanding of the information shortly and crisply. By doing so you will be showing the prospect that you are interested in his/her want and you have understood what they have said in detail. In case there is any misunderstanding, it is an opportunity for you to clarify the doubts with the prospect then and there. So, this is a very important technique to be used during probing.

Use Transformational Phrases

Generally, when you probe a prospect use transformational phrases. Transformational phrases are generally words that help the listener to transform from being a passive listener of a conversation to an active listener. Words like "excellent", "awesome", and "wonderful" are a few examples. Because when you use such words, you immediately perk up your listener. In selling, this means

- Your prospect will start listening more actively.

- Your prospect will get more involved in the conversation.

- Your prospect will believe that you are giving importance to their feeling and opinions.

- Your prospect's ego will be at its all-time high during the conversation.

- The conversation becomes more lively, interactive, and two-way communication.

This works wonders in both your personal and professional life, especially if you want to have a good relationship with somebody. But also remember, using too much of transformational phrases in your conversation can lead to trouble. People might think that you are mocking them, so be careful about how much of transformational phrases you are using. Don't overdo things at any given point in time.

Understand the Main Objectives of Probing

Even before you start the sales presentation you should be very clear on the flow of the presentation. The call control needs to be with you and not the prospect. During this stage of the sales presentation, you must be very clear about your thoughts on why you are probing the customer. The main reasons for you to probe the prospect or the suspect are as follows:

- To understand the want of the suspect/prospect/customer/ consumers.

- To build trust and a relationship with them.

- To understand the wants of the prospect.

- To understand what are the main driving factors that influence decision-making.

- Understand more about the suspect/prospect/consumers as a person.

So, when you are clear on the objectives of probing then ensure that you structure the entire sequence of the probing around that. Don't deviate from the set objectives.

Work on the Call Control

However hard you have worked and practised your sales presentations what happens in front of the suspect/prospect would change according to the individual and their mindset. Do not expect everything to go as planned; be ready for unexpected twists and turns during the sales presentation. There might be instances when you are probing, the customer might cut you short and ask you for the price. Now just because the prospect asked you for the price it would not be advisable for you to share any details of the price yet. Here, rather than sharing about the price, you can always revert by saying, "Sir, I will surely share more details on the price but before I do that I am sure you would also like to know more details on the product and its features and advantages and how beneficial it will be for you as an individual." The call control should always remain with you and not with the suspect or the prospect. Whatever happens, you need to know how to come back to where you were without disrespecting the suspect/prospect.

How Probing Helps

One of the main reasons for probing is to understand how best to develop the sales with the prospect. Everyone is different and the reason for buying a product differs from person to person. Why you think a prospect wants to buy your product may not be the same as your prospect's reason. For example, let's say as a real estate company, your company may believe that the main reason why prospects buy your apartments is for the amenities that are offered in the apartment. While that may be true, that may not be the only reason. For instance, let's say that a prospect has a child who attends school in that area, and he wants his residence to be not very far from his child's school, then the number of amenities that are offered in the apartment will take a backstage and the proximity to school will be the main reason for his purchase. Now all these things change according to the individual and their personal wants rather than a collective one. So while probing do not be too eager to jump to conclusions about the reason for the purchase. Keep probing until you are 100% sure about the suspect/ prospect's wants.

Don't Probe Only in Terms of the Product Requirement

Most successful sales personnel are those who probe well to understand the wants of the suspect/prospect/consumers, but many fail in this because they do not put in the effort to understand the individual more. So, it's very important as sales personnel for you to understand the requirements or the wants of the prospect and at the same time focus on understanding more about the likes and dislikes of the suspect/ prospect as an individual. Please understand that the individual is choosing to buy the product based on his/her likes and dislikes. Hence you need to work on understanding that part too. Before you complete the probing, you must have clear information on the wants of the suspect/prospect/consumers and at the same time, you should have more details about the suspect/prospect/consumers as individuals and their motivating factors to buy your product or the service.

Follow the Probe-Funnel Technique

The probe-funnel technique is the commonly recommended technique for sales personnel. Let's now look at what is meant by the probe-funnel technique.

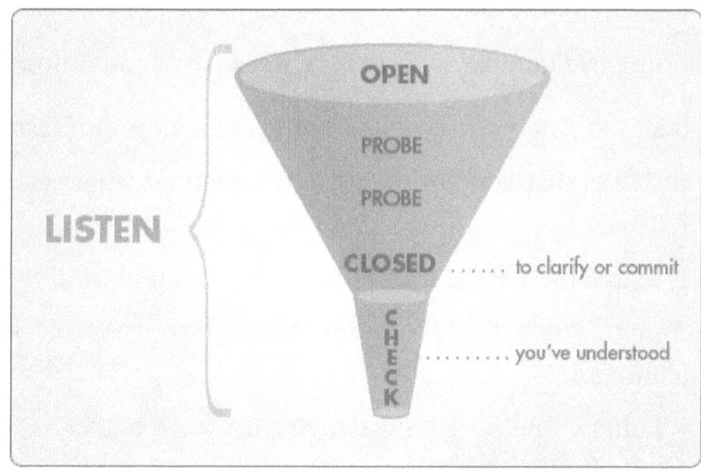

As depicted in the above picture, in this technique you start with open-ended questions while probing the suspect/prospect and you must continue to do so until you receive all the desired information. Then use close-ended questions to clarify if you have understood the information provided by the suspect/prospect correctly or to take a commitment to the information shared. Then paraphrase the information received from the suspect or the prospect and continue to the next probing question.

Maintain Eye-to-eye Contact While Probing

Maintaining good eye-to-eye contact with the suspect/prospect/consumers while probing is extremely important. This is easier said than done.

Generally, it's important to maintain eye contact with the other person 50% of the time while you are speaking or probing the suspect/prospect/consumer and maintain eye contact 70% if you are listening to a conversation. Also note that you need to ensure that you don't keep staring at the prospect, saying that you are maintaining eye-to-eye contact. Maintaining eye contact while probing helps you to stay focused on the information shared by the prospect; once you break the eye contact there usually comes a break in the flow of the conversation.

Maintaining eye contact is also done because of the following reasons:

- It shows that you respect what is being communicated.
- It shows that you are trying to understand what is being said and felt.
- It helps in creating a good relationship and bonding.
- It helps you to understand in detail your prospect's thoughts and feelings.
- It helps in building confidence from both ends.

Let the Prospect do Most of the Talking

This is the point where many sales personnel fail. They fail to understand that at this point in the sale presentation the limelight should be on the prospect and most of the conversation should be done by them. The responsibility of the salesperson is to ensure that this happens by using all the correct ways of probing and building a relationship with them. As a salesperson, you will have to ask the right questions using open-ended and close-ended questions in the right place to confirm or clarify and paraphrase what you have understood. Continue this until you have received all the information from the prospect. If you are doing right, then mostly the prospect will be doing most of the talking. Do not interrupt the person while they are giving you information or judge and prejudge a person based on the information that they are sharing with you. Remember, to be successful in sales it is very important to be a good listener first.

Rework the Probing Technique

Sometimes things don't work the way you want even if you are playing by the book. Many times, in my coaching class, young and upcoming salespeople come back to me with doubts like what they can do when a prospect does not have the patience to give us all the information if they are in a hurry, or simply not in the mood. Let me try to answer these.

The prospect does not have the patience to give us all the information: This could be because the salesperson would have jumped to this conclusion based on experience from a different prospect where they would have not followed the probing technique correctly, or they are just prejudging the situation or the individual.

The prospect is in a hurry, or they might get irritated: Firstly, understand that the prospect has given you time to come and meet them or they have come to your location to get more information on the product or service that you have to offer to them. That means they are showing interest. Now it's your responsibility to fan that flame and make them more interested. If probing is done properly, then such a situation would not arise. It is the salesperson's responsibility to keep the client interested. So don't jump to a conclusion or form an opinion too soon.

At this juncture, if you feel that you are not able to get the desired results, then it means you are not probing correctly. Go back to step number 1 in the selling process which is "Preparation" and write down all the probing questions that you have planned to ask. Stand or sit in front of a full-length mirror and practise asking the questions. Keep practising until you are comfortable and confident that you will do a good job in front of a prospect. You can even do a role-play with a friend or a family member to increase your confidence. Practise, practise, and practise until you are confident enough to sit in front of the prospect. All professionals become better over a period and so will you.

Provide the Company Description if Required

I would partially agree with this point that how much ever you are prepared reality might be different. Sometimes the customer might cut you short and ask you to give him/her more information about the product or service. Be prepared to handle such situations. There are two ways to handle tough customers:

- One is by telling the prospects that you understand their time is important and that you will get back to them as soon as possible with more details to provide them with the best possible options or solutions.

- The second is by acknowledging their request and start providing an outline of the company. Now be very clear that it is ok to provide an outline of the company's information if that's what your client wants. At that point do not start presenting your product's features, advantages, and benefits. If you do so you are not selling but you are only telling.

- There might be some prospects who might try to cut you short by saying that I know everything about your company and the product. Now, in this situation, I would recommend you use a transformational phrase and ask the prospect what he knows about the product or the company. Sometimes the best reply to a question is a question. For instance, "It's great to know that you know so much about our company and product. Do you mind telling me how you got this information?" I am sure you will be surprised to hear the response. The suspect/prospect will start interacting with you again. Try this out with utmost confidence and conviction.

Don't Jump at Every Opportunity to Present Your Product/Services

I have seen many people fail in sales or in convincing a prospect because they are not patient enough to follow the steps in selling as a professional. When they start probing, if some information rings a bell, they quickly jump to a conclusion about what the prospect wants and would immediately start presenting their products/services. This is a grave mistake and one that you should avoid like the plague. Even if the prospect has given you some information about his/her requirement, tell yourself it's better to get some more. Bide your time. Milk the cow as much as you can. Be it personal or professional information, try to elicit information as much as possible.

Be aware that the wants of the prospect might be different to the wants of the consumers of the products. So first understand if the prospect is also going to be the consumer of the product/service or if someone else is going to be the consumer. If there are additional consumers, then you need to probe and understand their wants as well. This is extremely important. Otherwise, your product will not reach the end user effectively.

Enough stress cannot be said of this one rule in selling: don't be in a hurry to present your products/services' features, advantages, and benefits before probing well to understand the requirements of your prospect and consumers if there are any. If you do so many times you will fail to convince the person that this product will satisfy their requirement. Sometimes out of sheer luck the prospect will end up buying the product or service. Please understand that you have not sold the product but still the customer has bought the product. Read the above sentence a few times before you fully understand the meaning of the sentence.

Selling is different from telling. If you can understand the wants of the prospect and then present the product in a tailor-made fashion to satisfy those wants, then it is called selling or else it is simply telling or demonstrating. Telling might also give you sales conversions but the conversion ratio is not something worth mentioning. Selling will always have a better conversion ratio than telling. I am sure that is what you would require as well. More sales, more incentives you get.

Chapter Summary/Key Takeaways

In this chapter, we saw the importance of probing, the dos and don'ts that are involved in probing, and the common mistakes by salespeople in this step.

Let's quickly recap what we learned on this topic

- Understood more about suspects, prospects, customers, and consumers.

- How to ask permission to start with a few questions?

- How and why we should use a white sheet of paper to capture information?

- Difference between probing and questioning.

- How to probe to understand the wants of the prospect?

- How to probe to build a relationship?

- How to keep the probing light?

- Importance of showing empathy for the prospect when required.

- How to listen to the prospect while probing?

- Why and how are we supposed to use open-ended questions while probing?

- How to paraphrase what you have understood?

- How to use transformational phrases while probing?

- Importance of understanding the main objectives of probing.

- How to work on the call control.

- Understanding how probing helps you to best develop the sales with the prospect.

- Importance of not only probing in terms of the product requirement.

- How to follow the probe-funnel technique?

- How and why we should maintain eye-to-eye contact while probing?

- How and why while probing, the suspect or the prospect should be doing 80% to 90% of the talking?

- How to rework the probing technique?

- Why we should not jump at every opportunity to present our product/services?

- Why we should provide the company description if required?

- Why we should not be in a hurry to present our product before probing?

In the next chapter, you will be learning about presenting solutions, another one of the most challenging steps in the selling process.

CHAPTER SIX

Presenting Solutions

In this chapter, we will be discussing in detail how to present your product/services to the prospect. As each step progress in the selling process, it becomes more challenging. So, your competencies should also be higher and better as each step comes. Till now we saw that it was the suspect/prospect who was doing more than 80% of the talking and as a salesperson, you only had to just introduce yourself and probe the prospect to understand their wants. Up until now, you have not done much verbal communication. Now the focus is shifted and going forward the entire limelight is going to be on you. The prospect along with the consumers are going to look up to you to see how best your product will be able to satisfy their wants and at the same time basis your interaction with them, they will also form an opinion about you and the company that you represent. So please understand that you are going to be carrying a lot of weight on your shoulders and there is going to be pressure on you. However, I urge you to enjoy this pressure, which will bring the best out of you. If you want to be successful in sales you need to know how to handle and enjoy the pressure. Until now, your skills as sales personnel have not been tested, trust me to form now they will be, so be ready for it.

Before we get into details of how to present the product let me explain why I have titled the chapter presenting solutions rather than presenting the product. Every prospect who is looking to purchase a product or a service comes because there is a need for him to fulfil; he has a problem, and he believes that problem would be solved by buying the product/service. This is true for all purchases. Now since there is a problem the prospect is looking to you to solve his problem with the solution you arc offering. And hence the title is focusing on presenting solutions rather than presenting the product.

Verbal and Non-Verbal Communication

As a salesperson, once you start presenting, everything that you say or don't will have an effect and you will be judged accordingly. Both you and your company's image will be defined by the way you interact with the prospect. So be careful and mindful about what you do. You need to focus on both verbal and non-verbal communication that you have with the prospect. Verbal communication is easier to master and control than non-verbal communication, which needs a lot of time and effort to be invested. The first thing the prospect notices about you is your posture while you are sitting or standing, so let us look at how to get this right. Good positive body language puts a person in a position of comfort, dignity, and likability.

- Get your sitting position correct. Most sales personnel don't concentrate on this but remember that you are being judged, so you better get this correct. While sitting on a chair, don't rest your back on the chair. You need to come in front and sit in a comfortable position and your back should be straight. Please don't hunch. If you are going to write something, then it's ok to bend towards the table that is in front of you, at other times you should sit with your back straight. Always ensure that you face the other person while speaking. Ensure that your shoulders are pointing toward the person that you are communicating with.

- While you are standing also ensure that you maintain a good posture, don't hunch. Ensure that your back is straight. Keep your foot parallel to each other and keep them pointed in front. Please don't have open feet while walking or standing as it looks very awkward.

- Maintain eye contact with the person you are interacting with. Follow the lighthouse technique while doing a group presentation. Understand that maintaining good eye contact shows that you are confident and not lying. It also improves understanding between individuals. It helps people to remember the communication along with creating attraction. Instinctively, people like and respect those who can maintain eye contact. It needs lots of confidence and practice to do this.

- Be careful about your facial expressions. You can understand a lot about a person from their facial expressions. Always be mindful of your facial expressions. Be sure that your facial expressions match the words that you use. The opposite will not be respected by the other person or group with whom you are interacting, as people can recognize what you are saying and that what you are thinking is different.

- Be careful with your gestures. Most of the communication happens between people nonverbally and gestures play a very important part in non-verbal communication. Be aware of the gestures that you are using during the presentation. A few examples of gestures commonly used would be waving, pointing, and showing a thumbs-up. Gestures can be broadly classified as voluntary and non-voluntary. Gestures are normally reflections of a speaker's thoughts, mostly hidden thoughts. So, you need to be very careful about this.

Verbal Communication

As I told you before now is the time to showcase all the skills that you have as a communicator. But it is also very important for you to understand what skills and attributes are required to be a successful and effective communicator.

- The best way to improve as a communicator is by practice. The more you practise the better you will become at communication. Watch popular orators, and how they started and refined their skills. In simple words, you need to practise your verbal communication regularly to be a good communicator.

- Control your ROS (rate of speech), which is the number of words that you can use per minute during your conversation so that the listener would find it comfortable in understanding or processing the information. ROS vary if you are speaking in your mother tongue or an acquired language. If both you and your prospect share the same mother tongue, and you are communicating in that language then you can use from 140 to 160 words a minute. If you don't, then I suggest that you maintain around 100 to 120 words per minute. Generally, there is a myth that if you have a higher ROS then you are a good communicator. It is false. If you have higher ROS than the suggested level the listener would not be able to process all the information passed on. Communication is not a running race, the speed at which you communicate does not count at all. It is all about how clearly you transfer the information to the other person and how well they have received the information that matters. So, a controlled ROS will always help. Now let us look at it with an example. Think about the best communicator that you have listened to, they can be from any walk of life like politics, TV show anchor, or sports commentator; the best communicators would be people with controlled ROS. Only if you have controlled ROS you will be able to modulate your voice as per requirement.

- Master your voice and modulate it as required. To be a good communicator you should know how to modulate your voice. More than the words, it is through the modulation of the voice, that the receiver fully understands the message. The change in voice modulation might change the entire meaning of the words many times. So more than the words the tone and modulation of the voice weigh higher in your ability to communicate. In very simple, voice modulation refers to how you control your voice while speaking. Effective voice modulation is the major difference between a good speech and a boring speech.

- There are normally four components to voice modulation which are referred to as the four P's which are pitch, pause, power, and pace. By now you would have understood that voice modulation is a key factor that will help you to keep the listener attracted to your sales presentation. So, it is very important to have good control over your voice and you should be able to modulate your voice well to keep the suspect/prospect/consumer interested in listening to what you have to say. Remember however good the product/service that you are selling is if you are not able to communicate well enough to the prospect he/she would not buy it. So more than the product it is due to the ability of the salesperson that the sales usually happen. In case you are not able to sell the product to a prospect then don't blame the company or the product/service that you are trying to sell instead blame yourself for the failure and inability to convince the person.

- Always be involved in the sales presentation and make it lively with your voice and your wit (occasionally). Even for a single moment don't lose track or focus, as I always keep repeating the call control should be with you and not with the prospect. The best of the sales personnel is a combination of excellent listeners along with being exceptional communicators. They are people who would make you listen to what they have to say even if you don't want to. Look for clues that are shared by the prospect both verbally and non-verbally. All information that you pass on to them or they pass on is very important in a sales presentation. So even for a minute please don't get distracted. Put away your mobiles during the presentation, and tell your colleagues not to disturb you during the presentation. Everything can wait until the presentation is over. At the end of the day, it is the customer who gives money to the organization to survive. It is the customer who gives money for your salaries and incentives whether he buys the product or not, give it all that you have got.

Presentation of the Product or Services Varies From Person to Person

I am sure by now you would have understood the difference between needs and wants. People buy a product or a service to satisfy their wants. So be clear each individual's requirements are different. Once you have probed the customer, the presentation of the product/service will vary according to the requirement of the prospect. The features and advantages will not change but the benefits will change according to everyone, so it is very important to focus on that. Everyone is different, some prospects might be egoistical, and a few might be emotional and so the presentation of solutions will also depend on the characteristics of an individual. If the prospect is an egotistical person you will have to do a lot of ego massaging, in case a prospect is an emotional person you will have to touch upon emotions while presenting the product/service. Surely, therefore, one stitch cannot fit all. You would be able to get all this information from the prospect only if your previous step of probing had gone according to plan, otherwise, things can quickly go south. It would then be an uphill task to convince the prospect to buy your product/service. When you deep dive into this if you are doing a B2B presentation or a family presentation then it becomes even more challenging as you will have to convince not only the customer but also the consumers as well. The customer sometimes might be an egotistical person and the consumer might be an emotional person. You need to be convincing everyone in one go. It is challenging, but if you are well prepared, you will be able to handle these situations easily. In case you are not feeling confident then go back to step number one in the selling process which is "Preparation."

I stick to the saying "if your sweat more at practice you will bleed less in war".

Understant the Want of the Prospect Before

Even though we have covered this topic in detail in the previous chapter there is no mistake in doing so again as you should now be convinced that if you do not probe the prospect well enough you will not understand the wants of the prospect. If you are not able to understand the wants, then how will you be able to convince them that the product/service that you are offering will satisfy their requirement? So even before you get into presenting the product ensure that you have understood the wants properly else get back to probing them again. In case you are failing in probing it's time to get back to preparation. It's like a simple flow chart.

Be Honest

This is one thing that I don't see in many sales personnel; most of them believe that they need to sell the product by hook or crook. I would completely disagree with them. Even if you manage in selling the product by lying to the prospect, someday he/she is going to find out the truth and all hell will break loose. Let us look at what will happen,

- The customer will lose confidence in you.

- The customer will lose confidence in your organization.

- The customer will start bad-mouthing you and your organization. Remember a happy or satisfied customer will go out and voluntarily spread the news in the market to less than five people but a dissatisfied customer will voluntarily go out in the market and share these problems with a minimum of 100 people directly.

- Remember the world that we live in is shrinking each day because of social media. In case the customer takes this up on social media your company's reputation would be at stake.

- There are chances that the customer might take a legal course of action against you and your company.

- There will be no more chances of repeat sales from that customer.

- There will be no more chances of cross-selling or upselling at any given point in time with that customer.

- There will be no more chances of reference selling through that customer.

- Please understand that selling through references is far easier than any other medium of lead generation.

With all this at stake, why would you want to lie to a prospect during a sales presentation? If you do so remember and be ready for the above to come true. I still don't understand why many sales personnel take that gamble and lie in their sales presentation. I would normally blame the managers and the sales heads if this happens in the organization and not the sales personnel. If strict action was taken against the perpetrator the first time, then it would have sent correct signals to all, and the entire team would never dare to do so. You would be able to know if the company or institution is playing along even after they know that the sales personnel are lying by looking at their cancellation of sales. In case this number is higher than the desired value then it is obvious that what I had stated is true. So please understand that lying in a sales presentation is nowhere acceptable, you might get a sale, but it is only temporary. You might have won the battle, but you will for sure lose the war.

Add Storytelling

A good storyteller is more successful in selling. Now don't get it confused with lying. They are two different things. Now let us understand this in detail, storytelling in sales is the art of presenting benefits to the customer rather than concentrating on the features and advantages. Understand that people buy a product/service not for its features or advantages but for its benefits. As we had already looked at, features are components in the product or service and when your features are compared to the competition and turn out superior to what the competition has to offer then the feature becomes an advantage and ultimately a benefit to the customer or the consumer. So, when you are presenting the features to the prospect it's advisable to touch upon the feature and concentrate on the benefit by using a story. It is also easier to convince a person by telling a story about how the feature will be helpful to them rather than by just talking about facts and figures.

Let us look at this with an example. Let us say that you are a salesperson who is selling real estate and you are responsible to sell an apartment. You are making a sales presentation to a family. Normally I see salespeople in these situations listing all the specifications and amenities that are present in the apartment like they are reading from the brochure. But is this selling? No. I would say that for every specification or amenity that is available in the apartment we as sales personnel will have to come up with a story on how that specification and amenity is going to be useful to the prospect. A classic example would be a swimming pool. I am sure that most builders offer a swimming pool as one of their clubhouse amenities. Let us now look at the presentation of the same by two sales personnel A and B—salesperson. A reads through the brochure and informs the prospect that there is a swimming pool which measures about 15 by 15 meters and also it is a temperature-controlled pool to be used in different weather conditions. Now salesperson B presents this feature using a story he says: "Sir/Madam, I understand that you have two children. I am sure they would love to go swimming often and I also do understand that because of your busy schedule you might not be able to take them outside to a swimming pool regularly. I know how it feels as this happens at my home too. Our apartment here has a swimming pool which is 15 by 15 meters in size which will allow your kids to enjoy their free time. We also have lifeguards present near the pool during working hours so that you need not worry about the safety aspects. Most importantly during holidays you need not step out of the apartment to take them out swimming. You can spend some fun relaxing time with your family during the holidays and create memories right at your doorstep. I am sure it is a very enticing thought. I would also like to share with you that our swimming pool comes with an all-weather controlling concept so that we will be able to adjust the temperature of the water in the pool according to the weather outside. This will ensure that the water is neither too hot nor cold and it will maintain an optimum temperature so that both you and your kids will have a wonderful time swimming together all around the year."

Now ask yourself which salesperson did a better job of explaining the feature of a swimming pool. I am sure hands down it would be salesperson B; don't you agree? He did not simply read about the features and amenities of the apartment from the brochure but he presented the feature using a story that would be enticing to the prospect. He knew about the prospect's personal detail, and his wants and he used that information in the presentation. Then he was able to paint a beautiful and realistic picture of the swimming pool that would help the prospect have a better lifestyle. So pitch your sales in a story format. Did salesperson B lie here? "No!" He simply presented the feature that was available in the apartment using a story that would relate to the prospect's life. Remember the story will change from prospect to customer. So, you need to be ready with multiple stories for different categories of people. The more stories you add to your sales presentation, the more you and your prospect will enjoy the presentation and your sales conversion will go up.

Now for you to be successful in storytelling you should have worked hard in step one of the selling process which is "Preparation." As you can see this is the most important step in a sales presentation. If you have not done enough of it, please go back to the drawing board again and again. Start preparing multiple stories for each feature and multiple stories for the same feature for different people according to their wants or lifestyle. Talk to your colleagues or senior official and learn from their experience.

Touch Upon Features and Advantages; Concentrate on Benefits

By now I am very sure that you would have understood the difference between features, advantages, and benefits. If you are not sure, revisit the "Preparation" step. You cannot be successful if you are not clear about the terminologies as all sales presentations revolve around that.

As sales personnel, be very clear about what your product has to offer—the feature, its advantages, and the benefits that the prospect will get.

Now the company or the product brochure will usually have enough information. As you read through the brochure for each feature, pause and present the advantages of that feature in comparison to the competition. By doing so you will clear all the doubts in the mind of the customer about the product and its superiority over its competition. As soon as you have covered presenting the advantages of that feature immediately get into presenting what is the benefit that the prospect would get out of the feature. Build a wonderful story around the feature, and present the benefit with all the emotions that you can bring to the table. Modulate your voice and work on your body language; it is these small things that count in storytelling. So, the better that you are at storytelling, the better you will be in sales. And tell a story that vibes well with the prospect to keep them interested and very importantly a story that would benefit them. Many times, I have heard sales personnel coming and telling me that they have tried storytelling in their sales pitch, but it has backfired and that they don't have the confidence to try it again as they both lost a deal and at the same time became a laughing stock. Why do you think something like that happened? Let's see some reasons.

- You would not have understood the wants of the prospect thoroughly while probing.

- You would not have presented the story with emotions.

- You would not have related the story to the requirement of the prospect and instead connected the story to someone else.

- Your voice modulation would not have been up to the mark and you would have not been able to bring in an emotional connection with the prospect and the story.

- Your body language would not have been great and would not have created positive energy.

- You would have told a story that was not interesting.

If you said yes to any or all of the above then your storytelling will not be successful. These are some of the reasons why storytelling sometimes fails during the selling process. Storytelling is an art and you get better at it with practice. To get your stories perfect please go back to step number one in the selling process which is "Preparation." First, write down the different profiles of people and the situations that you may encounter during a sales presentation, and come up with stories for each situation and profile that would match their expectations. Now once the stories are ready, practice in front of the mirror, once you are confident practise it with your family members and friends. Now, look at the difference after each attempt.

Create a Want For the Product/Service

As we saw already, a person coming in touch with a salesperson need not be a prospect. He could simply be a suspect, which means they have the need for the product/service but the want and the demand for the product/service might be absent. Now, this is a tricky situation to handle. In such a situation, when you realize that the person in front of you is a suspect rather than a prospect, don't get into presenting what your company or the product/service has to offer. Rather get into creating a want for the product or service. Let's say that you are a salesperson selling luxury cars and a person has come down to your showroom to enquire about the cars that you are selling but you are still not sure if the suspect has the appetite for luxury cars, the first thing that you will have to do is that you have to create a want for luxury cars in the suspect. Rather than selling the cars, convince the suspect that luxury cars are the solution that he is looking for. Once he/she becomes interested in what you are saying, then you can convince them that your company cars will be the perfect match for them. If you are not able to sell the concept of owning a luxury car to that suspect then there is no point in trying to sell your company's cars. If the want for the luxury car has not been raised, then where is the question of fulfilling that want? As we have already seen want and demand happen in a sequence. First and foremost, the need must arise, then the want for the product must arise, and only then the demand for the product/

service will arise. This works in a flow, if you try changing it you are destined to fail. Again, understand that you cannot create a need, you can only create a want and you can also partially create demand for your product/service.

I have seen salespeople fail miserably when they come across this situation because they directly try to convince the customer that the company and the product/service that they have to offer will satisfy their requirements. If you follow this, you will be successful in selling. Though you may not be able to achieve a 100% conversion ratio immediately, you will still be among the best and your conversion ratio will start improving day in and day out.

Never Knock Down the Competition With Below-the-Belt Remarks

While doing a sales presentation references made to your competitors will invariably crop up, either by the prospect or even by yourself to convince them that your product is the best in the market and that it is only your product that will satisfy their wants. Again, this is where many sales personnel get it wrong as soon as a prospect brings up the name of a competitor during the conversation the sales personnel would try to hit the competition with below-the-belt remarks and say that their product is inferior to what they are currently selling. Two reasons why you should not resort to such tactics:

- First, understand that only people who have something to hide or tell a lie or try to sell an inferior product/service will talk less about their competition and berate them unnecessarily. In life, if you notice, people who are confident and honest don't simply bad-mouth others.

- Let us say that you are working as a salesperson in a Hyundai showroom and a prospect comes down to your dealership; he wants to buy a hatchback. Now during the presentation, the prospect asks you about your competitors like Maruti and

Volkswagen and you immediately tell the prospect that they are not great cars when compared to your car. Think what would happen if the prospect already owned a Volkswagen and he is very happy about the build quality, performance and durability. He is probably there just to get a second car for his family. Do you think the prospect is going to trust you in whatever you are going to tell him further? Like you, many companies have loyal customers as well and they would not like it when their loyalty to a brand that they are happy and satisfied with is questioned. Now from the prospect's point of view, the following things will happen,

- He will lose the respect he had for you and your company.

- He will not believe in what you say.

- His ego would have been hurt as you have hurt his intelligence.

- He is not going to buy the product from you or your company.

- He will not recommend your product to his friends and family members.

- He may start bad-mouthing you and your company.

- You will never be able to build a personal relationship with the prospect.

- For life, he will not buy any product or service that your company has to offer.

All this happened because of one simple mistake that you did, you hit the competition with below-the-belt remarks or laughed at them; that is surely not the professional way to handle the competition.

When a prospect starts bringing up the competition during the presentation, he is happy that he is an informed prospect, and he is going to make your life easier. Don't laugh out or hit competitors with below-the-belt remarks, rather smile (don't laugh) and revert by saying that yes there are competitions in your business and that you are happy to have them in your space as well but go on to tell them why/how you are better and what you have to offer. By this time, I am sure you would have collected all information about your competitors during the first step of the selling process which is "Preparation", if you have not, again return to step one. Now start presenting each feature and then move on to present the advantages of that feature in sequence, and finally the benefit of buying your product or service. Add zest through some storytelling.

Confirm the Understanding of the Prospect

Once the tides of communication change, it is you, the salesperson, who will be doing most of the speaking and the prospect becomes the listener. To ensure that the message is passed on and received by the prospect as it is supposed to be, you will have to check with the prospect in a structured and repeated manner if he would like to get more information or if he wants anything clarified on things that you have shared about. Don't ask the prospect if he/she has understood what you have said as it would seem a bit rude. Instead, ask him/her if he/she would need more information or any further clarification on the same. If they say that they would need more information or if they request you to repeat the same thing once more do it with all the same passion, commitment, and conviction as you did before. Understand that the prospect is listening to this information as if it is for the first time, and whether they are subject matter experts or not, they are getting to know about your product for the first time. Understand that every individual's ability to process information is different and it will change with age and experience. While a youngster may understand better about technology, older people will be more concerned about safety features. As we know prospects are varied. When a prospect asks for repeated clarifications, it is your duty as a salesperson to set that doubt right. It is your job to provide information to the prospect and sell your product.

Work on the Call Control

Now as most of the verbal communication is happening from your end ensure that the prospect is actively listening to your communication and understanding it. Once you clarify the doubts of your prospect, make sure you come back on track to the same point of discussion you were doing before the doubts were raised. This is called call control or the ability to answer questions raised and to come back to where you were. To do this, you should be constantly aware of what you are doing or saying. If you don't remember what you were speaking about then you will be in trouble as the call control will not be with you and it will be with the prospect. The direction of the sales presentation will go as per the direction of the prospect which you must not let happen. Call control is not only the ability to come back to the point of conversation as it was after answering questions it's also the ability of the salesperson to take the flow of the sales presentation in a structured manner as he/she had planned. So, for you to be successful as a salesperson you should have the structure of the sales presentation and the sequence of the presentation planned well in advance and you should stick to it. I have seen many people fail in sales because once they lose the call control, they will be going as per the request or dictation of the prospect. Understand that the control should be with you and not with the prospect because you are the subject matter expert and being a professional you will know what you are supposed to say, when you are supposed to say it and how you are supposed to say it.

Relax and Be Friendly

Since the limelight is on you, there are high chances that you would feel tensed; it is ok to feel tensed and be put under pressure during a sales presentation. Even professionals have butterflies in their stomachs before their performance. Being nervous means that you are serious about what you do, and you want to give it your best shot. That said, however, don't allow the pressure to get to you. Keep reminding yourself to relax and that this is your performance time. You cannot lose it as you are well prepared. A word of caution here: relax, but do not be casual during the presentation. There are many differences between being casual and being relaxed.

When you remain calm and relaxed, you become friendly and approachable. It's easier to interact with those who are friendly and approachable rather than with those who are not, especially in sales, prospects always tend to buy more from people who are friendly and approachable. Being friendly and being friends are two different things; I am asking you to be the former. So, if you want to be successful in sales and if you want to increase your sales conversion ratio then you need to be friendly with your prospects. Only when you are friendly with them, they will feel at ease, and they will ask you a lot of questions and doubts that they have in their mind about the product/service. It is easier to create a rapport with a prospect by clarifying the doubts that have been raised by the prospect rather than the doubts that have never been spoken about.

Follow the KISS Philosophy

When you are presenting your product/services FAB, do it with style and ease. I have seen many salespeople trying to impress the prospect too hard. I suggest you follow the KISS philosophy here. In India, many salespeople believe that the full form of KISS is "keep it short and sweet", but the actual full form of KISS is "keep it short and simple" yes remember to keep your communication short and simple. Don't add too many jargons or terminologies that the prospect doesn't understand in your sales presentation. Be mindful of the fact that the prospect is not a subject matter expert as you are and many times, they will be listening to names and terminologies about the product/services for the first time in their life so it will be hard for them to understand and digest at the first time. So, keep it short and simple wherever possible. The best way to handle this situation is that when you use any terminology simplify it to the prospect. Don't assume that the prospect will understand or don't sideline it thinking it would be time-consuming, or that the prospect would not know about it. Let's understand this with an example and let's go back to the same example of working in a car showroom. As a car salesperson, you are asked to list the features of the car. Among the many, you also mention the RPM. But how many prospects know what is RPM? And some prospects for fear of looking ignorant, will not ask what it is. As a salesperson, it is your responsibility to make the prospect understand what RPM is first, expand it and tell how it makes a car go faster and why your brand of car is better because of this particular feature as compared to its competition. When you go the extra mile to make your client understand, you are already on the road to becoming a better salesperson.

Do Not Share Unnecessary Information

This is a grave mistake that is committed by many sales personnel. Eager to share information with the prospect many sales personnel tend to share information that is not required to be shared with the prospect. As a sales professional, you should know what to share and what not to be shared with a prospect. If the prospect asks for it, then it is your responsibility to share it. Else some things are better not spoken about. This might get you into trouble and might not help you in closing the sale or it might delay the closing of the sale. Let us look at some of the reasons why we are not supposed to share information that is not required.

- You might not be sure about how the prospect is going to respond to that situation.
- You might not have answers to questions that the prospect is going to ask you.
- Sales closures can get delayed or postponed.
- There are high chances that the prospect did not expect this.

Write Down What the Prospect Says

Remember that during probing I recommended using a white sheet of paper; I would again recommend you to use a white sheet of paper as a supporting tool along with the brochure while making a sales presentation. The paper should be used as a supporting tool and not as a replacement for the brochure or any other documents that the company recommends. The paper will allow you to control the call and it will show the customer that you are interested in his requirements and you want to help him to make the correct purchase decision. And write in capital letters. Why? Because

- Visibility is better

- Easier to understand

- Easier to recall

- Better look and feel

Be Clear on the Sales Flow

I have seen many people fail in selling because they are not clear about the structure and flow of the sales presentation. During the first step of the selling process, define how you are going to structure your sales presentation or sales pitch. I will share with you the most accepted way in which you can structure your sales presentation in sequence.

The structure changes from industry to industry and company to company. Let us look at how it is done normally:

Present your company details: While presenting your company information talk about the history of the company, the vision and mission, awards won to date and the track record of your company. Present information on how your company is different to your competitors and why the prospect should buy from your company and nowhere else. While presenting about your company do share information about the competition and what makes your company different when compared to your competitors. The prospect must be convinced to buy the product from the company that you represent as there is competition available nowadays.

Present your product: Once you start presenting the product don't be in a hurry to present everything in one go. Be clear on the structure. Know how you are going to take the presentation forward.

Touch upon the features: Now is the time that you will have to use the brochure. Start using the brochure and the white sheet of paper in front of you, and present the features that are there in your product/service.

Touch upon advantages: As you present each feature, present the advantages of that feature too as compared to the competition. This is where you show the prospect why it is very important for the prospect to buy from you and your company rather than the competition.

Present the benefits of the features: Once features and the advantages are enumerated, present the benefit of that feature to the prospect. Now is the time for you to do the storytelling that you have practised. Customize the presentation according to the prospect. Be very clear that you would be successful only if you are a good storyteller.

Chapter Summary/Key Takeaways

In this chapter, we saw how to present the product and the dos and don'ts that are involved in presenting solutions. We also saw the importance of presenting solutions in the selling process along with the commonly made mistakes by sales personnel in this step.

Let's quickly recap what we have learnt on this topic

- Why and how it is important to be careful about your body language?

- How to work on your verbal communication?

- How and why the presentation of the product or services varies from person to person?

- How to ensure that you have understood the want of the prospect before presenting solutions?

- How and why it is important to be truthful while presenting solutions?

- How to bring in storytelling in your sales presentation?

- Why it is important to touch upon features and advantages and concentrate on benefits.

- Why it is important to ensure that a want for the product arises and if it does not how to create a want for the product before presenting the product.

- Why it is important to never knock down the competition below the belt.

- Why it is important to confirm if the understanding of the prospect is on the same page.

- How to work on the call control.

- How to be relaxed and friendly.

- How and why to follow the KISS philosophy.

- Why it is important not to share information that is not necessary.

- How and why you should use a white sheet of paper while doing the sales presentation.

- How and why you should be clear on the sales flow.

In the next chapter, we will see in detail how to overcome objections.

CHAPTER SEVEN

Overcoming Objections

In this chapter, we will be discussing in detail how to overcome objections. As each step progress in sales, ensure that your skills are also up to the mark. At this stage of the presentation, having prepared well for the sales call, you have already introduced yourself to the prospect, you have also probed the prospect to understand their wants and then you have presented the product according to their wants too. Now however hard and perfectly you have done things till now, the prospect will invariably raise objections; just be ready for it and, in fact, be thankful that the prospect is raising objections. Many times, sales personnel feel that handling objections is very tough and prospects don't seem to be getting the point. I would say that yes, it is challenging to handle and overcome objections; yes, it is hard to convince the prospect that the product that you are selling is the right fit for the prospect. It's tough but not impossible. I am sure it is going to be challenging but if you need to be successful in selling then you should be prepared to handle these situations. Now let us look at how to handle and overcome objections once they arise.

Be Ready For Objections

Many times, I have seen sales personnel get into a defensive mindset as soon as prospects raise an objection. First, accept the fact that no prospect is going to agree to whatever you say. Second, start expecting objections. If you are mentally prepared and ready for objections to be raised, then half the battle is won. Don't get defensive as soon as objections are raised. Handle them rationally and objectively, don't let your emotions take over you. So, when you are ready for objection you will not be taken aback, and you will be confident to handle and overcome them. One of the problems that many sales personnel come across while facing objections is that they are not ready for it, they treat objections as a threat to the sales presentation or sales closures. Understand that they are not. Look at it optimistically or look at it as another opportunity that you have got to convince the prospect. I would suggest that you look at it as an opportunity for you to clarify the doubt that the prospect has. All of this would only be possible if you make a small change to the selling process or in your mind, and you start accepting the fact that objections are a part and parcel of the sales presentation.

Understand Why an Objection is Raised

When a prospect objects the most important thing that you will have to do as sales personnel is to first very clearly understand why the prospect is raising that objection, and why is he feeling that way. As many people say the best answer for a question sometimes is a question. So, when a prospect objects, revert by asking, "Sir/Ma'am can you please explain to me why you feel so?" or "Sir/Ma'am can you please tell me what the challenge is in this, according to you?" Always use open-ended questions. It is also very important to handle the objections very objectively without prejudging the customer. This is the most challenging part because most of the time when an objection is raised by a prospect the salesperson tends to jump to a conclusion based on his/her experience. If you want to be successful in sales or be a successful salesperson, understand that each and every prospect that you meet are different and each person has a different want. So you cannot give the same treatment to all customers. I would say "treat a prospect the way he wants to be treated".

But why does a prospect raise an objection? It could be because of various reasons:

- It can be because the prospect has not understood what you have told them.

- It can be because the prospect has misunderstood what you have told them.

- It can be because the prospect had learnt about it differently from someone else.

- It can be because the prospect would like to know more details about what you have said.

- It can be because the prospect has missed something that you have said.

Objections are raised for various reasons, not necessarily due to a mistake on a salesperson's part.

Start Probing Again

When objections are raised it is now your responsibility to start probing again. However, probe only that which is related to the objection or objections that were raised by the prospect. Write down the objections on the paper in front of you and note down the objection that was raised (take down hints and don't try to write the entire conversation). Listen to what the prospect is telling closely; in case you need more clarifications please ask him/her to share more details on that topic alone. Follow the steps of probing only on the objections the customer has raised. Don't get impatient, annoyed, or irate if the customer raises more than one objection. It is your job to handle and overcome objections and at the same time don't expect prospects to buy the product/service that you are trying to sell without a question asked. Don't get defensive about objections. See it as an opportunity to explain further your products/ services. When the prospect raises an objection, allow him to talk, and don't interrupt or tell the prospect what he/she is saying is not true. It is time to play the role of an active listener again. Listen and listen actively, probe, probe, and probe. The more information that you can get from the customer, the better it is better for you. This should be your agenda at this given point in time. Forget about everything else. The main mistake that many salespeople do is that they try to resell the features, advantages, and benefits to the prospect. Just don't do that. Instead, probe and understand the detail of the objection or objections that have been raised by the prospect.

Also, understand the feelings that are involved from the prospect's point of view. Many times, salespeople don't tend to understand the feelings of what is being communicated. They tend to forget that the prospect is as human as they are. The prospect also wants the salesperson to understand his/her emotions and feelings behind what he says rather than the words that are being communicated alone. You will be able to convince the prospect to buy the product or the service only when you can handle and overcome the objections that are raised by the prospect. If you are not able to do so then 99% of the time, you will fail to close the sales.

Objections are Requests for More Information

When you start probing without prejudging the prospect you will be able to understand that many times the objections are nothing but a request for more information. The prospect would not have understood fully the information you shared, or simply need more information. Sometimes it could be challenging as the prospect may not share a similar background and may need extra clarifications. Always put yourself in your prospect's shoes before jumping to conclusions. That will help you change your approach towards your prospect's objections. You will be more receptive and accept the fact that objections are a part of the selling process. If this happens then half of your battle in handling and overcoming objections is won. Now it becomes your responsibility to ensure that all the objections that are raised by the prospect are handled and overcome. Very importantly take time to explain all the objections one by one. Don't be in a hurry. Know that the learning and understanding ability of everyone is different and therefore, you need to alter your presentation from person to person. Avoid using jargon in your conversation and follow the KISS philosophy again. This is very important. In case you are using names and terminologies, explain each in detail to the customer.

Do Not Use the Word "But" While Handling Objections

Never use the word "but" while trying to handle and overcome objects. Let us say that a customer is raising an objection during the sales presentation, and you start by saying, "I understand what you are saying but let me tell you…" This is how many sales personnel respond. Let us look at the meaning of the sentence from the prospect's point of view:

- The salesperson is telling the prospect that his opinions don't matter.

- The salesperson believes that the prospect is not getting what the salesperson is saying.

- The salesperson believes that the prospect has not understood what the salesperson has said.

- The salesperson believes that the prospect has no understanding of what he/she is talking about.

- The salesperson is not bothered about what the prospect is telling.

- The salesperson is not willing to listen to the prospect's perspective.

- The salesperson is not interested in understanding the prospect's feelings and emotions.

Though the salesperson might have not thought about it this way, this is how the prospect would be interpreting your 'but'. This simple and small word can make or break a relationship. Instead of using "but" in your sales presentation rephrase the sentence, like, "I understand what you are telling me, now let me give you more details about the information that you are looking for…" If you want to be successful in selling never use confrontational words like "but" in your conversation with the prospect at any given point in time.

Avoid Head-to-Head arguments With the Prospect

On many occasions, I have seen sales personnel arguing with prospects while handling objections, sometimes as soon as prospects raise objections. This is completely unacceptable in sales. Please don't do it. Let us look at what is at stake when you argue with the prospect.

- You might win the argument, but you will for sure lose the sale.

- The prospect's ego would be bruised.

- You might have won the argument, but you will lose the personal relationship with the prospect.

- The prospect will look upon you as an arrogant individual.

- The prospect will start looking at you as an unprofessional and inexperienced sales personnel.

- The prospect will lose confidence in your company.

- The prospect will form a wrong opinion about the entire organization collectively.

Even if the prospect is wrong it is your responsibility as a salesperson to handle and overcome objections positively because it is your job. Understand that you are the professional here and not the prospect, so it is your responsibility and not that of the prospect. Also, the prospect is paying to buy the product or the service and so he has the right to share his/her thoughts about the product/service. As a salesperson, you are the professional who is trying to convince the customer to buy the product from your company, so it is your responsibility to handle and overcome objections in a very professional manner.

Work on a Constructive Discussion

Rather than arguing with the prospect, get into a constructive discussion with the prospect. First, be very confident about yourself, your company, and the product/service that you are selling. Be prepared. Don't be taken aback by what the prospect has to say about anything that you have told him/her or not during the sales presentation. You must be willing to go off the practised script, don't be very rigid in following the script. Understand that normally selling scripts are just a tool that will guide you through the sales presentation and you will never be able to follow the script word by word and if you try doing so you will fail in your attempt. Use transformational phrases during the conversation and allow the prospect to share what he/she wants to tell you fully, and please don't interrupt. Listen to what they want to tell you without interrupting and without any kind of distraction. Stay focused and show the prospect that you are completely focused on listening to what they are telling you. Show the prospect that you are concerned about them personally and it is very important for you to understand what they have told you and how they feel about what you have told them. Do not try to prejudge the prospect or what he/she tells you, it is not your job; your job and your responsibility are to bring in sales to the organization that you represent. Be very clear about that. You are no one to judge the intelligence of the prospect. Don't ever let awkward moments hurt you or take things personally. This is purely professional, and you will have to understand that. Don't let personal beliefs, likes, and dislikes affect your conversation. You are not here to make friends, although you should be friendly and professional. Show respect to the prospect, to what is being communicated and very importantly, about the feelings behind the words. Ensure that you have a controlled "ROS" (rate of speech). Don't raise your pitch or tone while communicating with the prospect. Actively listen. Allow the prospect to share all that he/she wants to share. Ask if the prospect has shared all the information, then paraphrase the whole conversation and check if your understanding is correct.

Come what may don't ever give up on trying to convince the prospect of the product/services FAB. Work on both your listening skills and verbal communication. Be careful about your body language it should go hand in hand with what you communicate. Take down hints on the white sheet of paper, this will show the prospect that you are interested in what they are telling you.

Understand the Difference Between Objections and Excuses

As a sales professional, understand the difference between objections and excuses. Many times, sales personnel do not understand this difference and hence they keep following up with prospects who don't buy the product/service, it is a waste of time. Many prospects will give you excuses, and they will try avoiding your conversation or follow-ups because they find it challenging to say no directly to a person who has treated them very well.

Let us look at both in detail.

S. No	Objections	Excuses
1	These are a request for more information.	These are given with the intent of escaping a certain point in time without displeasing.
2	These can be handled and overcome.	These cannot be overcome.
3	These are raised to understand more in detail about the company, product/services and what they have to offer.	These are told casually with the only intention of avoiding or taking the conversation further.
4	These are raised after understanding the product/services and its FAB.	These might be raised before understanding the product/services and its FAB.
5	These are raised by prospects	These are raised by suspects.

So both objections and excuses are very common in sales and if you want to be a successful salesperson you have to know their differences. If objections are raised then try handling and overcoming them, if excuses are raised don't waste your time and effort in trying to handle and overcome them, it is of no use.

Strike Off Objections That You Have Overcome

Remember I had asked you to take down hints on what the prospects are raising as objections. Now after handling and overcoming all the objections that were raised by the prospect strike out those that you have addressed on the paper. Why? After handling the raised objections when you strike off the objection on the paper it tells the prospect subconsciously that the raised objection has been answered. It also tells the prospect that the raised objection is no longer an objection, and he/she has understood the same. In sales, remember that it is very important to show the customer what you are doing. Sometimes it is what you show them that is more important than what you say. Strike out the objection only when you are 100% sure that you have handled all the objections raised by the prospect. Even if there is a minimal chance that the prospect is not convinced don't do that. Look for clues that the prospect will be sharing during the conversation it can both be verbal and non-verbal. Don't miss out on any information. Once you are convinced then strike it off on the paper.

Use Selling Tools to Handle and Overcome Objections

Use selling tools that are available in your tool kit while handling and overcoming objections. The tools would vary from industry to industry and sometimes even company to company. Sometimes there are common tools that can come in handy while overcoming objections let us look at what they are

- Calculators
- Brochures
- Price list
- Product availability chart
- Models of products sold
- Three-D miniatures of the products sold if available
- Laptops/Tabs

- Video presentation of the products

- Videos of the features that your product has to offer

Always remember that it is easier to convince the prospect using a tool rather than trying to convince the prospect through verbal communication.

Chapter Summary/Key Takeaways

In this chapter, we saw how to handle and overcome objections, and the dos and don'ts that are involved in handling and overcoming objections. We also saw the importance of handling and overcoming objections professionally and its importance in the selling process along with the commonly made mistakes by sales personnel in this step.

Let's quickly recap what we had learnt on this topic

- Why it is important to be ready for objections to be raised.

- Why we should start probing again.

- Why most of the objections raised would be requests for more information.

- Why we should not use the word "but" while handling and overcoming objections.

- Why we are supposed to avoid head-to-head arguments with the prospect.

- How and why we should work on a constructive discussion.

- Understand the difference between objections and excuses.

- Why it is important to strike off the written objections on the white sheet of paper.

- The importance of selling tools used to handle and overcome objections.

In the next chapter, we will see in detail how to close the sales.

CHAPTER EIGHT

Closing the Sale

In this chapter, let's see in detail how to close the sale. This is the most challenging step in the selling process, and this is the step where many sales personnel fail miserably because they just don't know how to close the sales, or they don't know how to ask for payment from the prospect after putting in so much of effort and time. Closing the sales will become easy if you know how to do it and at the same time it will become easier and simpler if you know what you are not supposed to do.

Before you get into this step be very sure about the fact that you have handled all the objections that were raised by the prospect and the prospect has also acknowledged the same. Don't be in a hurry to close the sales. If you have not handled and overcome all the objections there is no way the prospect is going to buy the product/service from you or get back into overcoming objections, and start all over again. Once you are 100% sure and confident that you have handled and overcome all the objections that were raised by the prospect then get into closing the sales.

What are the dos and don'ts that are involved in this process?

Closing the Sales Depends on the Prospect

The way you attempt to close the sale is completely dependent on the prospect and not you. To put it simpler, the closure of the sale depends mainly on what kind of personality the prospect is, whether, he/she is egoistical or emotional. Up until this point, you would have unconsciously gathered the kind of personality your prospect is from his movements, questions, gestures, etc. You will by now have a fair idea if he is driven by his ego or by his emotions. Without understanding this difference it is going to be very challenging to close the sale as the way to close a sale would differ for each. Now let us look at these two different types of people in detail I think this will help you.

S. No	Egoistical People	Emotional People
1	These people would want to know detailed information.	These people just don't like to get into detail. They believe understanding the outline would solve the purpose.
2	Mostly they show off that they are aggressive while they communicate both verbally and non-verbally.	Many times, they get defensive throughout the conversation.
3	They don't have any issues committing.	These people have commitment issues.
4	These people own up to their mistakes. They take ownership of it.	They don't own their past mistake. They tend to blame it on others.
5	They are mostly open and communicate freely with others.	They would be mostly silent.
6	They tend to exaggerate their abilities and achievements	They are not very comfortable sharing their achievements and abilities.
7	They find it challenging to empathize, they normally show sympathy.	They normally empathize with others.
8	They always feel that they are right.	They have to be motivated to believe that they are right.
9	They want more.	They are contended with what they have.
10	They don't accept failure.	They feel it is ok to fail.

Watch Out for Buying Signals

The next step in closing the sales is to watch out for buying signals from the prospect. Normally the prospect shares buying signals as early as during the handling and overcoming objections step. But you should know how to identify the buying signals. Buying signals are clues that the prospects give while interacting with a salesperson which indicates that he/she has decided to buy the product/service. Sometimes he/she even goes to the extent of visualizing owning the product or using the services and the benefits that he/she would get by doing so. Some of these clues may be given by the prospect verbally, and some non-verbally. Buying signals are different to commitments given by prospects so please don't get confused. As I told you already buying signals can be classified as

- Verbal buying signals
- Non-verbal buying signals

Let us look at both using examples.

S. No	Verbal Buying Signals	Non-Verbal Buying Signals
1	They use phrases like "I like it", and "sounds interesting."	They normally tend to smile and nod their head.
2	Asking for payment options.	Looking at the brochure for a long period of time.
3	Asking for more information on the warranty.	Looking at their companions and smiling at them.
4	Asking for delivery options and dates.	Actively listening to the conversation.
5	Asking for a trial if possible.	Picking their pen and playing with it.

The above-mentioned are just a few examples of both verbal and non-verbal buying signals. These signals should be considered only when they are passed on during the step of overcoming objections. In case you see this during any other stage of the sales presentation don't treat it as a buying signal and try to close the call at that juncture.

Closing Techniques

We already saw how closing the sales call depends on the type of personality of the prospect. Here are some closing techniques that you can use for the two different personalities:

- **The pen close:**

    o   This closure is recommended to be used for an egotistical person.

    o   In this technique, keep the booking form on the table and slowly take your pen from your pocket and ask the customer if he would like to use his pen or your pen to fill in the booking/application form.

- **The alternate close:**

    o   This closure is recommended to be used on emotional people.

    o   In this technique, you will have to give two options to the customer. For instance, if there's a choice of colour in the product you are selling, you could try to close by asking the customer by asking if he would like to go for white or black.

- **The challenge close:**

    o   This closure is recommended to be used on egoistical people.

    o   In this technique, you will have to throw a challenge at the customer if he/she is the decision-making person for the purchase. For instance, you could say, "I know that many people would not be able to decide on purchasing a product like this and of such value; so would you like to discuss the same with any of your family members before deciding?" This will goad the customer subtly to opt for closing the deal immediately.

- **The ego close:**

  - This closure is recommended to be used only on egoistical people.

  - In this technique, you have to concentrate more on the quality of the product or the service along with a premium charge for that, like, "I have normally seen only people who appreciate and are willing to pay an extra premium for the quality of the product purchasing this product. I am sure that you would agree and will be will go ahead with the purchase."

- **The negative close:**

  - This closure can be used on both egoistical and emotional people.

  - In this closure, you will have to tell the prospect that there would be a challenge in delivering the product/service instantly and there would be a waiting time for it. Let us say you are working for a car dealership you can probably say something like, "Sir, since there are already lots of booking happening for this model, we will not be able to deliver this model immediately. We will be able to deliver the car to you within 10 working days. Hope that is fine with you."

- **The guilt close:**

  - This closure can be used on both egoistical and emotional people.

  - You will have to make the customer feel guilty for not buying the product even if he/she must pay an extra amount of money for it. For instance, you can say, "Even though it might seem to be like spending a little more money than you had initially planned for we find many responsible people still buying the product because they know that they have no choice than to buy the product/service as it is the best option for their family too."

- **The sympathy close:**

  - This closure is recommended to be used only on egoistical customers. (I personally don't recommend using this closing technique, yet I am sharing this here because I have seen many sales personnel using this closing technique successfully during their sales presentation.)

  - In this closure, you will have to request to buy the product or services for your sake and assure him/her that it would be the best product that will suit his/her wants. Like, "I know that you have some reservations about going ahead with your purchase at this given point in time, but I have got to admit with you that as we are nearing the closing of the month, I am very desperate for this sale. I have been nominated for an award and this sale will surely put me in the driver's seat. Though you have some reservations I would like to tell you that this product is tailor-made for you and you will not regret the decision that you are making today. I assure you of that."

- **The puppy dog close:**

  - This closing technique is recommended to be used on egoistical people.

  - In this closing technique, you will leave it to the customer to make the call. For example, you can say, "I have covered all the points and I am very sure that this is the product that you are looking for and it will satisfy all your requirements. Now you will have to make the decision."

- **The last-ditch close:**

  - This closing technique is recommended to be used on emotional people.

  - This closing technique is supposed to be used as a follow-up attempt when other closing attempts have failed. When the previously attempted closure fails, and the customer says no to buying the product/service. Now as the salesperson leads the prospect to the door he/she pauses for a minute and turns towards the prospect and says, "Sir, I would like to say one last thing to you, I am very sure that this is the best product that will satisfy all your requirements. I feel very guilty that I am not able to make you understand this and I am not sure where I went wrong. Can you give me one more chance to explain things to you and let's see how it goes on from there?"

- **The pros and cons list close:**

  - This closure can be used for both egoistical and emotional people.

  - This closure is also recommended to be used as a follow-up to a failed attempt to close a sale. In this closure, as soon as the first attempt fails you will have to tell the customer, "I understand that it is a tough decision to make, and I understand that there are a few things that are stopping you from deciding. To clear those doubts let us do a small activity." Even as you are saying this pull out a white sheet of paper and place it in front of the prospect. Divide the white sheet of paper into two halves and ask the customer to tell you what are the things that he likes about the product and what is stopping him to make the decision. Ensure that all the positives are written on the left side of the paper and the points that are stopping him from deciding on the right side of the paper. Start with the positives and keep writing them as hints and in capitals. If you feel that he has missed something, remind him of that and ensure that he accepts them. Once he has covered then move on to the points that are stopping him from making the decision. Don't interrupt, and once the list is done handle it like objections and clarify those doubts. Once you have completed the activity hand over the white sheet of paper to the prospect and tell him sir yes, I see that there are a few things that are stopping you but look at how many things you like about the product, in case you are not going ahead you will lose a lot of things.

- **The elimination close:**

  - This closure can be used on both egoistical and emotional people.

  - This is similar to the pros and cons close but with a slight difference. This closing technique will also be used as a follow-up technique when your first attempt to close the sales fails. When the customer declines to buy the product or service, place a white sheet of paper in front of the customer and request him/her to tell you what the points that he/she feels are stopping him/her from making the decision. Once you have written them, it is your time to go back to what you did while overcoming objections. Treat all the points that are stopping the prospect from buying as objections. Handle all the points one by one and once you have convinced the prospect immediately strike it off the list. This will make the prospect feel that point is no longer a stopper. Cover all the points that were raised by the prospect one by one.

- **The ultimatum close:**

  - This closure is recommended to be used with emotional people.

  - In this closure, you would have to offer a hard situation for the prospect to deal with. Like you can say, "Sir, please don't forget that this is the last day for the offers to end. In case you are not able to decide by today, I regret to tell you that we will not be able to offer the product/service at this cost again."

- **Cost of ownership close:**

  - This closure is recommended to be used with emotional people.

  - In this closure, you don't focus on price, instead, you have to focus on the total cost of the ownership of the product or the service and the benefit that the prospect would receive in return and then you would go on to compare the overall cost of the ownership offered by the competitors.

- **Daily cost close:**

  - This closure can be used on emotional people.

  - In this closing technique, you will have to present the overall cost of the product by showing it as the cost of ownership per day and tell the prospect that all that he would be paying is x number of rupees for a day and get so much in return.

- **Quality close:**

  - This closing technique is recommended to be used on egoistical people.

  - In this closing technique, you have to emphasize the quality of the product and not the price. You can talk about how the prospect will feel about owning a product of that quality which not many people would have and tell him how others will look up to him for owning that product.

If t Does Not Work...

Sometimes the closing of the sales may still not happen despite trial closing. When that happens, go back to objection handling and overcome all the objections that are raised. Don't expect the prospect to buy the product from you instantly or within one attempt. He/she will have concerns and it is your responsibility as a salesperson to clear all the doubts in the mind of the prospect and convince them that they are making the correct decision in buying the product from you and your company. The product/service will be bought by the prospect only when he/she is convinced about all the features, advantages, and benefits of the product. And this will not happen if the prospect is in doubt about even one single aspect. So to reiterate, it is your responsibility to make the prospect understand all these points in detail.

Practise Doing Different Trial Closures

As the saying goes "Practice makes a man perfect", it is very important for you now to get back to step no one in the selling process which is "Preparation." Put in a lot of effort to understand what kind of a person the prospect is. Once you have done so, then practise different closing techniques for different personalities. Practise with confidence how you will make them feel comfortable while asking them to pay for the product or the service. Many salespeople, while they may excel in other steps fail miserably when they come to this last step. Finally, you should be able to ask the customer to pay up for the services/product he plans to buy from you. If you cannot, then the whole point of sales is moot. Being a good demonstrator will not help you in being a good sales presentation because you will have to understand that at the end of the day the company and your manager are going to be looking at how many sales that you have brought to the company rather than how well you demonstrated the product/service to the prospect. Remember, your success in sales will completely depend on your ability close more sales and not on your ability to make excellent sales demonstrations. Being an exceptional sales demonstrator will not guarantee you great success in sales.

When you try closing techniques, explore more than what is mentioned in this book. I have mentioned only a few. There are many more available. Read more and more about topics related to this. Once you have penned down the trial closures that you are comfortable with sit in front of the mirror and start practising them one by one. Concentrate not only on what you are doing but be very conscious of how you are doing it. Concentrate on both verbal and non-verbal communication. As I have always told you the most important part of communication is not what you say but how you say it. Once you are confident about attempting good sales closures it is time for you to attempt doing it with your friends and family members. Request for their time I am very sure that they would help you. Try doing sales closures according to the individual and after that ask them for feedback and work on it. Don't take offence to the feedback because it came from your friends and family members, understand that they are trying to help you out. Look at it rationally. Take their feedback as if it was shared with you by a prospect.

Don't Be Pushy

Many times, in sales even after giving your 100% and giving your best performance the prospect might not be able to make a buying decision over the table and there might be many reasons for it. Let us look at a few reasons:

- The prospect would need more time to think and decide.
- The prospect would like to discuss the buying with his/her family members.
- The prospect would look at considering different payment options.
- The prospect would like to consider a few other options in the market.
- The prospect would like to see what the competition has to offer.

The above-mentioned are a just few of the reasons why the prospect might be buying time to make the decision, don't blame the prospect for doing so. Put yourself in the prospect's shoes before jumping to a conclusion. Do not push too hard. Many times, I have seen sales personnel pushing the prospect way too hard to close the sale then and there. Closing the sale on the first attempt is not your objective, closing the sale is your objective. Again, this is where many sales personnel lose their plot, they tend to push the prospect way too hard to make the decision then and there. He might just end up saying no to you. Once the prospect says no, then it will be an uphill task for you to recover from that. So, rather than pushing the prospect way too hard, it is always better to give the prospect the time that he/she requires

Chapter Summary/Key Takeaways

In this chapter, we saw how to close the sale and the dos and don'ts that are involved while closing the sale. We also saw when to attempt a trial closure, what to do if the trial closure fails in the first attempt, how to do it in a professional manner, and its importance in the selling process along with common mistakes by sales personnel during this step.

Let's quickly recap what we have learnt on this topic:

- The closing of the sales depends on the prospect.
- The importance of watching out for buying signals.
- The different types of closing techniques that you can use.
- What to do in case trial closure does not work.
- The importance of practice doing different trial closures.
- Why the salesperson should not be very pushy trying to close the sale?

In the next chapter, we will see in detail how to follow up better in a sales call and its importance. Not many sales personnel tend to give this lot of respect and importance it deserves. There is no way that you will be successful in selling if you don't get this step correct.

CHAPTER NINE

Follow-Ups in Sales

Unfortunately, this step is not given the kind of importance that it deserves in the selling process. It is looked at as if it is a very easy thing to do in the selling process. Let me assure you that it is not. If only salespeople understand why this is important and what are the mistakes that many do during this process, they will offer the kind of respect that this step deserves. Many salespeople fail in closing the sale or in sales because they don't follow up well with the prospect. In this chapter, we will look at how to follow up better in a sales call and how to do it professionally.

Taking an Appointment for the Follow-up

Many times, during the closing sales presentation, the prospect would need more time to decide on buying the product or service. As a salesperson ensure that you get an appointment with the prospect for the follow-up. Many salespeople tend to leave the customer premises without fixing up an appointment for a follow-up. It is a fatal error in sales. It is easier to fix an appointment with the prospect while interacting with him rather than trying to follow up without an appointment with the prospect. It becomes an uphill task to follow up with the prospect without an appointment and it is also not professional doing so. I have seen many people not able to close the sales because they would take this step in the sales presentation way too lightly.

Follow-up as per the Appointment Date and Time

Stick to the appointment date and time. Here many sales personnel fail because they don't give importance to the appointment date and time. They tend to follow up but not according to the date and time that was given by the prospect or in simple terms they will miss the appointment time given by the prospect. By doing so there are high chances that you would lose the sale and the relationship with the prospect. Further,

- They will think that you are not a professional.

- They will think that you don't understand the value of their time.

- They will think that you are not giving them the importance they deserve.

- They may even meet another salesperson from a different company and consider buying that product or service in case that salesperson did a better job.

- They might even go to the extent of forming a bad impression about your company as a whole.

So, it is very important for you to follow up with the customer as per their availability and not according to your convenience.

Don't Start Conversation Business-like

During following up with the prospect make sure you don't start the conversation about the business directly. Such a business-like attitude will not endear you as a salesperson to the prospect. During a follow-up meeting, the prospect will expect some familiarity. So before you meet the prospect recollect all the information about the prospect. Ensure that you get all the facts correct. Use technology or even good old dairy to write down about each prospect and their requirements. There are even many advanced software to help you maintain a log. Your company even may have one of its own. Even if your company does not provide this support, it is your responsibility to ensure that you buy a software subscription that would give you solutions for your requirement. Don't look at this as an expense but rather an investment. This data is as important as gold for sales personnel. Once you have recapped all the information about the prospect and the details, he/ she shared with you, now it becomes your responsibility to use the information with you to your advantage and start the conversation.

As already mentioned, don't start the conversation diving directly into the business. Start on a lighter note, but don't be casual or disrespectful. If the prospect's family had come for the first meeting, you could enquire about them. Even if they hadn't but if the prospect had mentioned his family or children in the first meeting, you could start the follow-up meeting by enquiring about them. Build a rapport with the customer, to a level that he/she would trust you and share more personal information about him without any concerns. However, spend no more than a few minutes discussing other topics. Once you have broken the ice, get on to business.

Be Professional

As a salesperson, respect your prospect's time. Every professional should do it. If you want to be successful in sales be respectful of your client's time. In turn, your prospect will respect you. If you are tardy, your prospect will not trust you or your product/service as he may doubt all that you have told him/her about the product and the company that you represent. If an emergency arises and you know you cannot keep up the time, do inform the prospect and request him/her for an alternate time. Again the best way to handle a client is to always put yourself in his/her position and see how you would react in the given circumstances. Understand that the prospect is also as human as you are. You will have to understand that the prospect is giving you an appointment at his/her convenience and not yours. He/she understands his/her life better than anybody else. So, when he/she is giving you an appointment they would have taken a lot of things into consideration like his personal and professional commitment and after weighing in all the options. This will enable you to be a successful salesperson.

Get to Know the Personal Likes and Dislikes of Prospects

During the earlier part of the sales presentation, the prospect would have shared a lot of information with you. It can be about his/her personal or professional life, or it can be about his likes and dislikes.

Use all the information available to you to your advantage; talk about things they like and are fond of. Don't touch upon things that they don't like, or are uncomfortable with. Use all the information available to you to your advantage. When you start talking about business it is also important for you to understand the likes and dislikes of the following people

- **Customer**: The person who is going to pay for the product or service.

- **Consumer**: The end use of the product or service.

- **Influencers**: The people who will play a vital role in the decision-making of the prospect.

- **Gatekeepers**: The people whom you will meet first before meeting the customer. They are more prominent in B2B selling, e.g.: Secretary.

In sales, though the customer is a very important person it does not mean that you can neglect others.

Know Your Prospect's Important Personal Dates

During your sales presentation make sure to get personal information about the prospect, like their date of birth and wedding anniversary. Or dates that are important to them and use them to your advantage. If for instance, any of these dates fall before the date of your appointment with the prospect feel free to call the prospect and wish them, or you could send them some flowers or a cake. Understand that you are building a relationship with a prospect. But not every prospect would become your customer, so don't go overboard with your gifts and embarrass the client. Ensure that the rapport you build with the prospect will make them come back to you to buy the product/service. There might be instances where the prospect would not be able to buy the product or services from you at a given point in time because they would not have the demand (both the ability and willingness to pay) for the product or service. It is ok. It would eventually happen. Don't get disheartened.

It's a part of the selling process. Things take time. You can be aggressive in trying to close the sale but at the same time don't be desperate for a sale. When you become desperate you will lose control and finally, end up losing the sale. So, use the information that is available to your advantage in the follow-up meeting and build a good personal rapport, trust, and bonding with the prospect.

Use Family Information Wisely

Use the information about the prospect and his/her family to your advantage while following up on sales and while trying to close the sale. Prospects love to talk about their children. If you are privy to such information, especially if the prospect has kids below the age of 12, they will surely love to talk about their children. Remember their names and ask about them in the follow-up meeting. For example, let's say your prospect has two children, a son and daughter aged 12 and 9 respectively and their names are Rahul and Meghna. You can start the conversation by asking, "Sir, how are Rahul and Meghna doing? Hope schools have resumed for them." This is more effective and personal than simply asking, "How are your children?"

If you were in the prospect's shoes, which will build more trust and confidence in the salesperson? I am sure that you would agree with me that it would be the former.

Now let us understand this from the prospect's point of view. When you had used common terms like son and daughter the prospect would appreciate the fact that you have remembered them but the personnel connect will not be built as they are common terms used to refer to anyone's children. Whereas when you specifically mention the names of the children in your conversation you connect better with the prospect. As a parent, the prospect would respect you for remembering his children's names and enquiring about them. A word of caution here is to remember the names right. It would do you no good to get the names wrong and fumble afterwards. If you forget it is always better to simply address them as children.

Address all of the Prospect's Concerns and Objections

There would be occasions in sales where you would not have an answer to the question or objections that are raised by the prospect while doing a sales presentation. So, the best way to handle those situations is by being honest with the prospect and telling the prospect that you don't have the answer to that question at that moment, but you will get the required information and share it with the prospect soon. Don't think that the prospect will look down on you; in fact, the prospect would respect you for being honest. They will also respect you for accepting that even though you don't have some information presently, you are willing to come back with the answer soon. They will definitely respect you for not trying to push the prospect into making a buying decision while they still need more information or clarifications on the product or services sold.

Now when you come across these situations seek help from your colleagues or higher officials on that topic. Try getting the answer from them and go back to step one in the selling process which is preparation. Understand that you will have to be preparing yourself daily to be successful in sales, don't feel bad about it. Once you have all the information speak to the prospect again and move on as we had discussed in "Overcoming Objection". In case you are meeting with the prospect for the second time after collecting all the required information on the objection raised by the prospect during the first conversation then start the follow-up conversation as we had discussed until now and they get to the information that the prospect has asked for. Build the conversation around that topic and treat it as another objection and overcome it. As you are handling that objection again start looking for buying signals and once you spot a buying signal try doing a trial closure as we had discussed in the chapter closing the sale. Ensure that all the objections that are raised by the prospect are handled and overcome before you move on. Don't try doing a trial closure while the prospect still has any doubt in his/her mind.

Close the Sales Only After Overcoming Objections

Once you are very sure and confident of the fact that you have handled and overcome all the objections and clarified all the doubts in the mind of the prospect on the product/services that you are trying to sell it is now the time again for you to try closing the sale. Be aggressive in sales, but not desperate. Now treat this situation as a new sales presentation again, look out for buying signals, both verbal and non-verbal.

Once you have identified a buying signal from the prospect it is your responsibility to do a trial closure again. In case some more objections arise go back to overcoming objections and then come back to doing another trial closure. Yes, it is challenging but it is also rewarding being in sales. It is a war, psychological warfare. A conversation between you and the prospect will go around in circles for few times and then it would reach the point that the final decision must be taken by the prospect. Once you have reached that point don't wait or hesitate in asking for the payment. This is where many sales personnel fail, they get defensive, or they are not that very confident in asking for the payment. This is the moment that you have been waiting for and worked hard for until now with the prospect. Take confidence from the fact that until now you have put in your best efforts and you are sure that the product will satisfy the wants of the prospect and that the product or service that you are selling is the best that is tailor-made to satisfy the want of the prospect.

Now again go back into closing the sale. Close it using the various techniques enumerated in the previous chapter depending on the personality of the prospect.

Practise, practise, and practise. You will get better with experience. No one is born a successful salesperson they all evolve as successful sales personnel. Sales is a professional job, respect it and don't be in a hurry. If you want to be successful in sales, you will have to be patient and willing to learn. Haven't I already said, "Rome was not built in a day"?

Ask For references:

Despite your best efforts, there could be two possible outcomes:

- The prospect would buy your product or service

    Or

- The prospect would say no to buying the product or service

Whatever happens from here understand that you have given it your 100%, and don't expect every sales presentation to convert into a sales closure. As a salesperson, it is your responsibility to ensure that you put in your best efforts and try to convert all the enquires into a sale without prejudging a prospect. At the same time be mentally prepared for the fact that all enquiries will not convert into a sales conversion. This is the hard truth. Whatever might be the outcome, ensure that it is your responsibility as a salesperson to ask the prospect or the customer for references. Now be clear I said both prospects and customers. That means you should ask both kinds of clients—those who are your customers and those who finally said no to you.

Why asking for references is important? Because

- It enables lead generation.

- The cost of lead generation by references is far lesser when compared to any other marketing medium.

- Conversions of sales are far higher in leads generated through references than in any other medium of marketing.

- It builds a better brand image.

- Profits for the organisation increase as spend on marketing decreases.

- It builds on loyal customers.

Now I am sure that you would understand the importance of asking for references from all your prospects and customers. Generate more leads and do name-dropping, especially of the person who provided you with the reference and start the conversation from there. It would become easier and simpler for you in sales. Since the lead was passed on to you by a prospect or a customer they will act as a brand ambassador for you and your company so half your battle is won even before it started.

Chapter Summary/Key Takeaways

In this chapter, you would have clearly understood in detail how to follow up in sales and the dos and don'ts that are involved while following up in sales. You would have also understood the importance of asking for references and how to generate more leads and sales from each prospect and customer that you interact with. Let us now quickly recap on what are the topics that we have learnt in this chapter.

- Why it is important during closing the sales, we should never leave the prospect without making an appointment for a follow-up.

- Why it is very important to follow up as per the appointment date and time without fail.

- Why we should not start your follow-up conversation with the business.

- Why following up as per appointment is an indicator of the salesperson's professionalism.

- How and why it is important to understand the personal likes and dislikes of prospects.

- Why it is very important to get to know the prospect's date of birth/ wedding anniversary.

- How to use the information on children available to you wisely.

- How to ensure that you answer all the concerns and objections that were raised by the prospect before attempting to close the sale?

- How to close the sale after handling all the objections raised by the prospect.

- Why it is important to ask for references.

Conclusion

When I started writing this book, my only objective was to transfer the knowledge that I had gained over a period of being in sales and training and development, training many salespeople to get better at what they do. I wanted to share this knowledge with more people and help them to get better at selling and have a successful career in sales. As I promised in the beginning of this book, when you finish reading this book, you will transform into a confident and complete sales professional. I am sure that we would have achieved the goal that we had set for ourselves which is to be better sales professionals.

Now that you know what, when, how, where, and why we are supposed to do things in selling, I would like to emphasize the why part. I am sure as professionals we will do things the way it is supposed to be done once we have the answer to the question of why. If you cannot answer the "why", then you cannot consider yourself to be a professional. I am sure this book would have given you enough information on the why part.

Now I would like to throw some caution to the wind. I would like to remind all my readers that just because you have read this book does not mean that you will be transformed into a better salesperson overnight. What you now possess is adequate knowledge to be successful. Having that knowledge is just one part of it. You now need to use the knowledge to your advantage and start practising what you have learnt in the field with your prospects. Before that practise with yourself and then with your family and friends. The more you practise the better you will become. Understand that you will get better with time. Remember the saying "the more you practise in peace the less you will bleed in war".

There's a lot more to learn about selling to be successful but I would assure you that these are the fundamentals that you will have to be first very clear on before you want to get more information and knowledge on selling. What is the point of having great interiors inside the house if your building's foundation is not strong? These are the fundamentals of the selling process once you are clear on this we can work on more aspects in the future.

I would also to request and remind all my readers to read this book at least a couple of times so that you would understand all the details mentioned in it clearly. It might sound simple to be executed but trust me when I tell you this, it is not as simple as it may sound.

Practise, practise, and practise your sales presentation. Remember **"Not every sale is successful, but everyone can be a successful salesperson."**

References

I have used liberally various terms and technologies as described by Dr. Philip Kotler, the Father of Modern Marketing.

I have also used the **Wikipedia,** the free online encyclopaedia, created and edited by volunteers around the world and hosted by the Wikimedia Foundation. This platform has provided so much information on topics related to sales, marketing, human behaviour, and an explanation of terms and terminologies that are used in sales and marketing, which I have borrowed as references in this book.

Pictures that are used in this book are taken from the internet for explanation and illustration purposes alone.

About the Author

Srinivas S N is an alumnus of IIM Calcutta and a hotel management graduate. He has more than six years of experience in sales and more than 14 years in training and development. He has worked with companies in training and development like Club Mahindra, Airtel, The Lalit, and Casagrand. His last employment was with Casagrand as a VP, Training and Development. During his tenure in training and development, he has designed and redesigned processes for various organizations and helped them to achieve their business goals.

After helping many organizations achieve success, he decided to pursue his ambition of starting his own company and launched "Azpirehi Business Solutions" in 2018. This company has got into two verticals which were Sublimation Printing (absprints) and Business Consulting Services (Success Dimensions). He ensured that both those companies achieved great results in the past four years and maintained good growth even during the testing times of Covid. Recently he also went on and Co-founded "Thiram Sports Academy" one of Chennai's largest multisports training academies and a sports infrastructure development company.

Apart from this, Srinivas S N is also an active Youtuber who runs his own channel named "Success Dimensions" which offers guidance on how to run a business successfully. This is a Tamil YouTube channel.

Srinivas has offered training and consulting services to top companies like

1. Navins
2. Casagrand

3. Radiance

4. GSquare

After quite a lot of consideration, Srinivas decided to offer consulting services for SMEs and start-ups. He believes that these companies are the ones who would require more consulting when compared to reputed and settled organizations. He is currently working towards his goal which is to help, support and guide a minimum of 100,000 new start-ups and SMEs by the year 2030. He believes doing this will not only help in ensuring that these organizations achieve business success but it will also help India as a country achieve its dream of becoming the largest economy in the world.